▲▲▲

THE
SOUTH SOUND
USER'S GUIDE

Edited by **Ken Miller**
Illustrated & Designed by **Sean Alexander**

South Sound Press, Tacoma 2012

Library of Congress Cataloguing-In-Publication Data
Miller, Kenneth, 1947 –
The South Sound Users Guide/Ken Miller and Sean Alexander
p.cm.
ISBN: 978-0-9882910-0-3

1. Travel – tourism 2. Pacific Northwest of the United States
– Washington State – South Puget Sound.

First edition, 2012

For Janet; lots to do!
KRM

For my folks.
SPA

Contents

Foreword

As the South Sound Users Guide staff brainstormed and developed the concepts for this inaugural edition, one theme, one question, repeatedly influenced their thinking: Why here?

There are a few no-brainers: the natural beauty of the mountains and the interconnected waterways; the seasons, four real seasons; the relatively modest standard of living.

Beyond those answers, though, there's a pioneering spirit that draws and keeps us all here. Walk into a South Sound coffee shop — one that embodies espresso fanaticism and a small corner dedicated to local beer, of course — and breathe in the social circles. Fretting over water rights or parking costs you'll find a montage of liberals and conservatives, natives and transplants, off-road addicts and tavern-hoppers, grandpa sweaters and vintage dresses, letterpress printers and camouflage pants on a mid-afternoon Americano break — all cooking up some kind of hustle. You can wash up here friendless and in no time at all find yourself enmeshed in an entrepreneurial enterprise with 20 of your new best friends — three-fourths Tweeting updates.

Until the Mountain comes out.

If you can see Rainier the Macbooks fold, the backyard chickens head into their pens, the civic-planning degrees and quilt projects go on hold and in a half-hour the bike's back off the car and you're grinning, through breath-takingly lovely and tree-engorged Rainbow Falls, Capitol Forest or Kapow-sin. If a big happy dog stuck his head out the car window, maybe you end up at Owens Beach or Nisqually Refuge, Kopachuck or Potlatch State Park.

In the small cooler, go-local road sodas and gluten-free pretzels and Odwalla bars and organic turkey sandwiches. There's a Bluetooth connection loaded with dirtystupidfun '80s hard rock and badass garage rock and Mahnhammer and Vicci Martinez and Basemint.

Then back home while it's still light – it's light very late out here – and the neighbors are playing catch with the kids or sitting on the porch with beers and there's a spot for you.

The mystique of the South Sound, it unifies. It is at once powerfully individualistic and also the great equalizer, the uniter of beliefs and political agendas and lifestyles and clothing choices, appealing across the board to Repubs and Dems and antique dealers and drywallers and Lesbian pickled asparagus canners exporting to Asia.

Almost everyone loves the view. With or without the big loping beautiful dog in the picture, it's a veritable Viewmaster of postcard awesomeness.

The South Sound offers options. Tasty options. Refreshing options. Reinvigorating options. Ridiculous and possibly prosecute-able options. Take advantage of the many options in the pages that follow.

By way of confession to readers already here: the term "staycation" often popped into my head while penning this introduction. I don't think I said it out loud and so it quickly devolved from fairly apt to cloying. But honestly, I can't be sure. So if I said it, my sincere apology.

Oh, and one last note. If you do go deep into the woods, remember: bears can smell minty toothpaste from miles away and reach speeds up to 35 mph...

Ron Swarner, *Lifelong South Sounder*

The South Sound from 30,000 Feet

The South Puget Sound has 1.1 million people, 3,000 square miles and three counties. Pierce, with about 800,000 people, includes Tacoma, the region's largest city. Thurston County has more than 200,000 people and includes Olympia, the state capital. Mason County is less developed; Shelton is the county seat.

Getting Around: The region is easy to reach by air, rail, and road. Water access is feasible but not so easy.

Seattle-Tacoma International Airport (SEA) is among the 50 busiest airports in the world and ranks fifth for on-time departures. Except for heavy fog in December, local weather almost never disrupts air travel. Olympia and Gig Harbor have general aviation facilities.

AmTrak runs from San Diego to Olympia and Tacoma; the main route is the romantically-named Coast Starlight. Trains connect at Portland and Seattle with all major points in North America.

U.S. Interstate 5 [I-5 in local parlance] runs north from San Diego through Olympia to Tacoma; I-90 from the east connects with I-5 just north of Tacoma.

While no cruise lines reach the South Sound at this writing, Pacific sailors have access through the Strait of Juan de Fuca, on the southern end of Vancouver Island. The South Sound offers lots of moorage and maintenance facilities.

Cycling is relatively safe. Major streets have bike lanes, and well-maintained trails cross much of the three counties.

Public transportation is improving but hasn't achieved the frequency or scope common in very large [or transit-forward] communities. There is bus service from SeaTac Airport to Tacoma and Lakewood, and an infrequent bus between Tacoma and Olympia.

Cabs are not common and more reliably called by phone, not hailed from the curb. While a car isn't essential, it makes a short visit easier.

Weather and Wear: The Cascade Mountains divide Washington State into east and west. Puget Sound is said to be on the wet side, the dry sort of joke in vogue around here. There *is* a drip; it's rainy 150 days of the year. But there are no more annual inches than Miami, say, or Kansas City. The rain is just more spread out. And helps plants stay green.

Snow is quite rare, as are days over 80 [F]. The air tends to be pretty clean; burn bans are in effect some days but this should only affect visitors using wood stoves. Caps are common for men and women; the frail may use umbrellas.

This is a relatively informal part of the world. Khakis and polo shirts or sweaters are appropriate almost everywhere; jeans and tee shirts not so much but passable. There is, however, no South Sound version of the formal aloha shirt or *guayabera*; business is still done in business attire, whatever that means.

The Peeps: The South Sound is happily diverse. While the region is mostly white – and of the white people, heavy to Scandinavian in origin - people of color make up about a quarter of the population.

Native American place names dominate the area. The only really challenging one is Puyallup; it's pronounced PEW ahl lip. Native lands dot the three counties, inhabited by people from a dozen tribes and bands.

There are large numbers of people originating in the Pacific and Asia, Central and South America, the former Soviet bloc and Africa.

Gay men and lesbians are pretty comfortable in the South Sound. The area has long affirmed their rights. Common sense is always in good taste, of course, particularly in less populous areas.

Unlike Seattle, which has one of the nation's lowest kid populations, the South Sound is child-friendly. The school year is the traditional nine months with winter and spring breaks. Summer is packed with activities, especially outdoors.

Socially, low-key pleasant is the default position. People tend to say hello, don't yell in restaurants or stare. Unless there's yelling. Nor do they flaunt their differences. It's not blending in as much as being different together and allowing each other a little space.

Sounding Local: As mentioned above, interstate freeways [5 and 90] are called I-5 and I-90. Local freeways are called by their numbers alone, as in "take 705 to..." We generally don't say "the Five." This is speaking Californian.

The University of Washington is You Dub; denizens are Huskies or Dawgs. The Evergreen State College is Evergreen; students and alum are Greeners. Washington State University is Wazzu and has Cougs [Cougars]. University of Puget Sound is UPS; Pacific Lutheran is PLU; St Martin's University is Saint Martin's.

The Seattle Seahawks tend to be called the Seahawks, win or lose. The Mariners are the M's; winning not so common lately. Seattle used to have a professional men's basketball team called the Sonics or Soops [SuperSonics]; mourners remain active. Women's basketball: the Storm. The soccer team is the Sounders.

Tacoma is T-Town to hipsters; Olympia may be Oly but not so much.

Mount Rainier is the regional icon; when it's distinctly visible people say, "the mountain is out" or "did you see the mountain this morning?" A knowing nod is the correct response. Puget Sound is "the Sound."

"The" or "a" Chihuly refers to a work in glass by Dale Chihuly [chih hoo lee], a Tacoman. This is not a generic name for glass art; other glass is by other people. Rhododendrons are rhodies. There are over a thousand known species including azaleas, so if a flowering plant is hard to identify, there's a decent chance it's a rhodie.

Fort Lewis and McChord Air Force Base merged recently; the new nomenclature is JBLM [Joint Base Lewis McChord]. It covers almost 150 square miles [plus a training base in Yakima], has 35,000 active duty troops and 15,000 civilians. This is one of the country's major military installations and the Army's only "power projection platform" west of the Rockies.

The state is Washington; the national capital is Washington D.C.. Vancouver tends to mean the city just north of Portland; Vancouver B.C. is the city just north of the U.S..

Food, Drink and Smoke: Every region has its signature items and the South Sound is no different. First is seafood, served fresh. Really fresh, like it needs a good slap. Salmon compete with Mt Rainier for regional symbol. The L [in salmon] is silent.

There's lots of local produce. Berries are distinctive, with root crop shipped all over the world. Rhubarb is abundant [see Sumner].
Some beef and pork are grown locally; local poultry is available including in lots of back yards. Well, not exactly available; one should ask the home-owner.

Locally-roasted coffees, local wines – some with area grapes – and micro-brewed beers are all growing rapidly. Many food places have vegetarian and vegan menus as well as sensitivity-sensitive items, gluten-free and more.

Asian restaurants are common, including Thai and Vietnamese, Korean, Chinese and Japanese. It's easy to find good Mexican food. The index lists restaurants by type of food.

It's illegal to drink alcohol on the street or in a vehicle – driver or pas-senger. Being drunk in public is not cool, even in demographics that think it is. The drinking age is 21. Beer, wine and distilled spirits are now sold commercially except for two a.m. to six a.m.. Schedule accordingly.

Smoking tobacco in public spaces is illegal; this includes near the entries to buildings. Marijuana laws are a little confusing at the moment, but public use is certainly illegal.

Safety and the Streets: Litter is frowned upon; recycling and separation of waste are civic virtues.

Runners and skateboards are not uncommon on city sidewalks; pedestri-ans usually yield. Bicycles tend to stay off the sidewalks.

Many intersections are unmarked, especially outside the downtown cores; drivers should yield to the right. Pedestrians and drivers often see cross walks as suggestions; pedestrians should not assume drivers will stop.

As elsewhere, drivers are expected to yield to the right and stop or pull over when emergency vehicles approach. Letting buses merge is a good idea if not mandatory.

The Washington State Patrol is responsible for freeways; police and sheriffs patrol other roads. In the highly unlikely event of a volcanic eruption, lahar emergency routes are marked in potentially-affected areas.

The emergency phone number is 911.

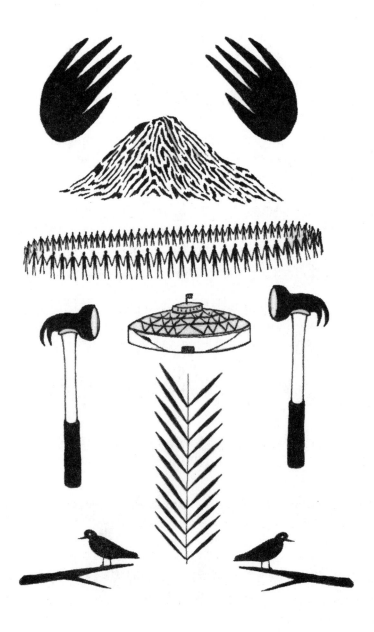

How to Use This Book

Our book is called the South Sound Users Guide for a reason. We didn't write a guide for driving through the region and taking pictures out the window. We envision people climbing out of the car and experiencing the South Sound: eating the food, hiking the trails, ooh-ing and aah-ing as glass blowers defy danger one more time.

Using the place, in other words. Not in the sense of exploitation but like we use a glass to drink water or a pencil to write notes: to meet a need. In this case, to meet our need for fun and wonder.

To that end, the Guide is organized on two principles.

First, we list only unique, local features. We're not necessarily against global coffee places or retailers with a thousand locations; but we're focused on what's different from Dubuque or Dubai. That's what interests us and we hope interests our readers.

Second, we think geographically rather than by topic. The book is structured by place – Tacoma's Theater District, for example, or Tumwater – rather than by type of attraction like art galleries or hotels.

The first geographic sort is by county: Pierce, Thurston and Mason. These form the book's three main parts.

Then within each county are "hubs," about 40 of them. Tacoma and Olympia each have several hubs; other communities – Yelm, Sumner, Allyn – are hubs in themselves.

Finally, within each hub are "features" – specific attractions like trails and burger places, museums and shops. The Guide has almost 800 features; they're the heart of the book. Generally we have not included services for residents like dry cleaners or service stations, but when a service is absolutely distinctive we've written about it. These are few.

Most of the hubs have maps, with numbers corresponding to the features so readers can see which streets are crowded with features, or which corner to turn to find a specific spot.

The description of each feature includes a physical address, a telephone number and a web address when available.

The features aren't rated for quality or appeal. They're in the Guide because they're worth a visit. The unworthy don't get a low rating; they simply don't get in. And there's no paid content in the Guide. The text comes from the judgment of the writers and editors.

Hours of operation are not included because they change, and can be found on line. The same is true of menus and ticket prices.

The index reverses the logic of the book; it ignores geography and shows features by type. So a reader looking for French food can find it in the index [food, French]; similarly the index lists all the hotels and B&Bs under "accomodations."

Thanks to Brian Forth and Sitecrafters, the Users Guide has a way-finding application. This allows users to make their way from one feature to the next or search for features by type. For information on how to download the free app, write sswayfinding@gmail.com. The way-finder is a great companion to the Guide itself; thanks Brian!

There are no bad seats; pick a page and c'mon in.

Errors and Omissions

Mistakes have been made.

The South Sound Users Guide is a collaborative effort among a lot of people, but ultimate responsibility is with the editor, a human.

When we saw a mistake we fixed it but we almost certainly missed things. Some are minor, like a mis-placed comma. But a few could ruin the morning, like listing an address on North Meandering Drive instead of South.

We checked and double-checked. We really did. But almost certainly we missed something. Please accept our apologies in advance.

In addition to these errors of commission, it's likely we failed to include some cool places. Very likely. At some point we simply had to stop writing and go to press.

So here's our hope: readers who find mistakes will tell us. And readers who have suggestions for making the Guide better will tell us that too. The best way is by email, at guidebookfeedback@gmail.com.

If you send us feedback of any kind, you can get the next edition of the Guide at a deep discount. Thanks!

Geocaching

Thanks to backer Jeff Helsdon, the Users Guide has a geo-caching challenge named, aptly, the Helsdonian. At each of five sites you'll find a cache with coordinates for the next step and a log-in. To begin the Helsdonian, you'll need to travel back to the base of time near 47.272,-122.488877. This can be a hazardous journey; look both ways. And if you see Jeff, say thanks.

▲▲▲

PART ONE:
PIERCE COUNTY

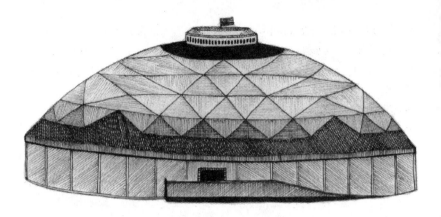

Tacoma's Dome District & Eastside

This is a great starting point for a Tacoma tour, a regional transportation hub and a nubby, walkable neighborhood in its own right. The district features entertainment, retail, dining, and history as well as connections for buses, trains and light rail. The neighborhoods are home to some of the earliest residents of the area - the Puyallup Tribe – as well as recent immigrants, providing a rich, diverse view of Tacoma's people and cultures.

Erica Coe, John Hines and Kim Thompson

The LeMay – America's Car Museum

The largest private car collection in the world; that's what the Guiness Book of Records called the late Harold LeMay's 3,000 + vehicles. And in June 2012 America's Car Museum opened with LeMay's collection at the heart of a four-story experience. About 300 cars – and motorized vehicles of all kinds – are on the main show floor at any one time. Most are from the core collection but others are on loan from private collectors and institutions around the world. On the ramps from floor to floor are specialty exhibits like classic Indy race cars or experiments in alternative propulsion. Those ramp examples illustrate

two important dimensions of the Museum. Exhibits like the old Indy cars take care of the "ooh" factor, that gasp when we turn a corner and see legends brought to life. But there's also the "oh" factor, the "I didn't know" element at LeMay. Vehicles can be a lens to help us see science and culture and history, and one of LeMay's great ambitions is to interpret the world this way. In the coming years this aspiration may lift LeMay from the top tier of car museums to the level of the finest museums in the world. Interpretation is a work in progress, but off to a fast start.

Meanwhile back on the ground,

the four floors include a ten-screen theater [think the chase scene in Bullitt], race car simulators, slot car racing, a cafe and gift shop and a hang-out for classes and car conversation. Outdoors: the Haub Family Field, almost four acres of grassy concourse. Car-club gatherings, festivals and concerts are slated here. [Asleep at the Wheel performed on the Museum's opening weekend; other aptly-named bands to come.] LeMay is open seven days a week, with discounted admission for students, military and seniors; kids under five are free. Special rates for groups and schools.
• 2702 E D St.
• 877.902.8490
• lemaymuseum.org ❶

Speaking of vehicles, day parking is free at the transit station. Express buses leave from here to Lakewood, Olympia and SeaTac airport; Sounder train service also heads north. **The Link Light Rail** is also free and makes convenient stops: University of Washington and historic Union Station in the Museum District; the Convention Center; and finally the Theater District. • 424 E 25th St. • 888.889.6368 • soundtransit.org/Rider-Guide ❷

The Tacoma Dome
One of the largest wood-domed structures in the world, capable of seating up to 30,000, the Dome's interior features neon art by Ste-

phen Antonakos. Events cover a wide spectrum from professional and amateur sports to trade shows and blockbuster concerts.
• tacomadome.org ❸

The Shanaman Sports Museum of Tacoma-Pierce County
Attached to the Dome between the lower level A doors and the Exhibition Hall, the Museum tells the rich history of local sports. It's named for Fred Shanaman, a fine amateur athlete himself and strong advocate for team and individual sports in the South Sound. The Museum includes the Washington State and Pierce County Halls of Fame.
• 2727 E D St.. • 253.272.3663
• tacomasportsmuseum.com ❹

Brown and Haley
This historic candy company delights customers around the world. Its classic confection, Almond Roca, was created in the 1920's and keeps morphing new varieties. The outlet store offers distinctive gifts.
• 110 E 26th St. ❺
• 253.620.3067 • brown-haley.com

Crystal Voyage
Billed as a "spiritual oasis," the shop encompasses a large metaphysical book section, crystals, candles, oils, and altar pieces. In business since 1987, this isn't about gimmicks. Staff and guests offer classes and special events.
• 2601 E D St. • 253.272.4367
• crystalvoyage.com ❻

Tacoma Book Center

With 16,000 square feet of retail space, Tacoma's largest used book store. The store is well organized, the staff helpful.
•324 E 26th St. •253.572.8248
•Tacomabookcenter.com ❼

Freighthouse Square

In the heart of the Dome district, century-old Freighthouse Square is an indoor mall of local merchants and food vendors including Thai, Indian, Mexican, fresh pastries and a half dozen more. The Square covers three city blocks. Free parking.
•2501 E D St. •253.305.0678
freighthousesquare.com ❽

Strawberry Hill

Historic homes from the turn of the century – the late 19th - dominate this walkable neighborhood. Chosen by This Old House Magazine as one of the nation's best places to buy an historic home. Bounded approximately by McKinley and East L, East 30th and East 34th, just above McKinley Park. ❾

El Gaucho

Special-event dining at one of Puget Sound's most storied restaurants. Fresh seafood, aged beef, exceptional service, outstanding wine list. Live music nightly; private rooms.
•2119 Pacific Ave.
•253.272.1510
•elgaucho.com ❿

Alfred's Cafe

This family friendly restaurant offers generous portions of American fare at good prices. And excellent mixed-drink values. ⓫
•402 Puyallup Ave. •253.627.5491

Friesenburgers

Great burgers, kids' and gluten-free menus. Bison and vegetarian burgers, salmon.Dine in or take out. Open late for special events.
•308 E 26th St. •253.203.6753
•friesenburgers.com ⓬

Celebrity Cake Studio

Family-owned by third-generation bakers, at work since 1999. Custom cakes of course but also fresh goods including pies, cupcakes, wheat- and dairy-free items. Often comes out on top of "Best of…" lists. Home of the Cake-Mobile. •314 E 26th St. •253.627.4773 •celebrity-cakestudio.com ⓭

Tacoma Tactical: The Airsoft Center

Airsoft is like paintball but with foam pellets instead of paint. The pellets go pretty fast. TacTac has 20,000 square feet under cover as well as outdoor space. The focus is CQB: close quarters battle. Open weekends. • 1625 E Portland •253.345.8282 •tactac1.com ⓮

Emerald Queen Casino

Tacoma's pre-eminent gambling · destination. Regular entertainment

includes comedy, music and boxing. Restaurant and buffet open late. Smoking allowed inside; no minors. • 2024 E 29th St.
• 253.922.2000
• emeraldqueen.com **⑮**

Portland Avenue Park
The park shares a site with the Community Center. Rugby/soccer fields, playground, restrooms, sport courts, wading pool, and a picnic shelter. Totem Pole at entrance.
• 3513 Portland Ave. **⑯**

online information for this and other Tacoma parks can be found at metroparkstacoma.org; use the "Park Finder" under "Facilities".

Stanley and Seaforts
Killer views, reliably good food and excellent service. That about runs the table for a special-meal place. Classic American menu with seasonal variants. The lounge is popular for working meals and just stretching out. Reservations recommended; ample parking and valet.
• 115 E 34th St. • 253.473.7300
• stanleyandseaforts.com **⑰**

Portland Avenue
Frog and moon street light standards and salmon and canoe bus shelters connect the art of the historic Coast Salish residents to the contemporary community.
• E 29th St. & Portland Ave.

McKinley Park
Considered one of the most beautiful parks in Tacoma. Contains playgrounds, picnic areas and sport courts along with open areas for dog walking.
• 907 Upper Park St. **⑱**

Top of Tacoma Bar and Cafe
Voted best bar in Tacoma by readers of a local weekly. Good food, relaxed environment, reasonably priced. Bread, most produce and much of the meat is organic and local. This is a happy blend of foodie place and neighborhood bar. Covered outdoor seating; pool and video games including Big Buck Hunter, Safari Edition. Dude!
• 3529 McKinley Ave.
• topoftacoma.com **⑲**

Story Salmon
Part of the Soul Salmon Project to raise salmon awareness through artist interpretation, this is one of several salmon sculptures around the city. • 3888 E Portland Ave.

The New Frontier Lounge
A hidden gem that is worth the trip across town. The New Frontier features the best in indie rock and eclectic booking nightly.
• 301 E 25th St. **⑳**

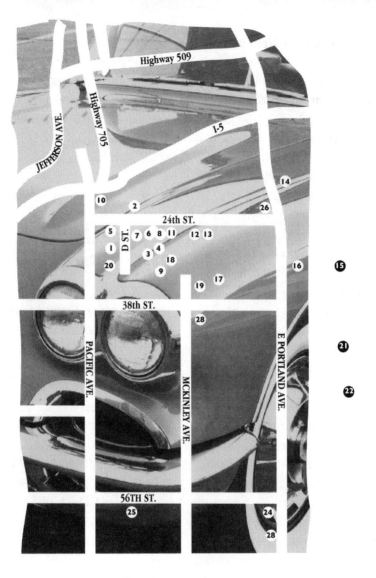

Salishan Gathering Place

Redmond's Pomegranate Center worked with community members to design this community hub. World War II shipyard housing was cleared away and a new community built largely with private funds. The copper was salvaged from Union Station and the granite came from Tacoma streets. • 2203 E 42nd St.

Swan Creek

This undeveloped canyon and stream provide a close-in respite from city life. The 290 acres are crisscrossed with trails and popular with walkers, picnickers and people out to explore some urban wilderness.
• 2820 Pioneer Way E
• 253.383.2429 ㉒

Portland Avenue Nursery

The park-like atmosphere alone is worth the visit. This full scale nursery has been locally owned for 25 years and is dotted with old tools and miscellany kids enjoy. Knowledgeable staff. Dog friendly.
• 1409 E 59th St. • 253.473.0194 ㉓

Blueberry Park

This park provides five types of blueberries free for the picking during the summer months. Much of the park is taken up with fields and wetlands, but it does have a playground and paths.
• 7402 E D St. ㉔

Tacoma Soccer Center

The area's largest indoor soccer center with leagues and classes for all ages. Drop-in and pick-up soccer at night. Recently renovated fields and spectator seating.
• 2610 Bay St.
• 253.906.7856
• tacomasoccercenter.org ㉕

Cloverdale Park

Often overlooked, Cloverdale has basketball and tennis courts, picnic facilities, playground and walking path. • 1635 E 59th St. ㉖

Stewart Heights Playfield and Pool

Large park includes sports fields, walking trails, tennis courts, and a skate park. Recent renovations have vastly improved the facilities. The "pool" is an understatement; this is a water park, with water slide, Lazy River, zero-depth entry, bubble pool and water play structure as well as a large outdoor pool. The park is open year-round and is free; the so-called pool is open during the summer; full and half day passes are available; children 4 and under are free.
• 402 E 56th St. • 253.573.2532 ㉗

Tacqueria el Antojo

Popular and authentic Mexican restaurant. Reasonably priced good food. Breakfast.
• 3801 McKinley Ave.
• 253.475.0375
• taqueriaelantojo.com ㉘

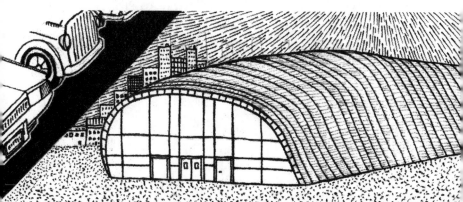

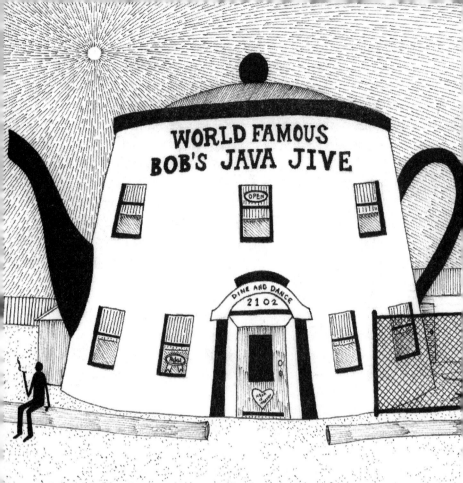

South Tacoma

The community was first developed as the site for the Northern Pacific Railway shop. Employees soon settled close to work and brought their families. The area holds onto its working class persona and offers unique opportunities for visitors.

John Hines

Wapato Park

Dominated by its namesake lake, Wapato Park includes large open spaces for exploring flora and fauna. Historic pergola and garden, sports fields, picnic facilities, and a paved walking trail around the lake.
• 6500 S Sheridan Ave. ❶

Gateway Art Project
Fritz Church

Commissioned to commemorate the role of the Northern Pacific in the beginning of South Tacoma. Gateway to the Water Ditch Trail and Tacoma Cemetery.
• 4745 South Tacoma Way

Tacoma Cemetery

This historic cemetery is considered one of the most beautiful on the west coast. The resting place for prominent citizens who have given their names to many streets and parks.
• 4801 South Tacoma Way
• 253.472.3369
• newtacoma.com ❷

South Park

Manicured trails and gardens and the South Park Community Center. Picnic facilities, sports fields, play equipment, an auditorium available for rent. Connects to the Water Ditch Trail.
• 4851 South Tacoma Way ❸

Tacoma Mausoleum

First mausoleum built west of the Mississippi. Adjoining cemetery contains the Civil War veterans who relocated to the area. On the National Historic Register.
• 5302 S Junett St.
• 253.474.9574 ❹

Stonegate Pizza and Rum Bar

This is the place for pizza in the South End. Full menu and an adjacent rum bar. The pizza takes time but is worth the wait; includes a gluten-free crust and veggie toppings as well as the uh, *un*usual like Peanut Butter & Bacon.
• 5419 South Tacoma Way
• 253.473.2255 ❺

Northern Pacific Bank Building

The historic building was the home of the bank for workers of the Northern Pacific Railroad Shops.
• 56th and South Tacoma Way

Coming Home, Larry Anderson

Bronze sculpture commemorating Tacoma's centennial and South Tacoma's connection to the railroad workers and families. In front of Heritage Bank. • 5450 South Tacoma Way

Heritage Bank Mural, Mary Mann

Located in the parking lot behind Heritage Bank. • 5445 S Washington St.

Marcia's Silver Spoon

A South End fixture known for its simple setting and large breakfast portions. Biscuits and gravy, good hash browns, that kind of place. Reasonably priced menu in a cozy environment. Early birds beat the wait. • 2601 South Tacoma Way
• 253.472.0157 ❻

Wapato Hills

One of the last wild spaces in South Tacoma, this park contains trails for runners and walkers and open space for bird watchers. And in an unusual melding with structured play, there are baseball and basketball facilities, a playground, a sprayground, and picnic areas. • 6231 S Wapato St. ❼

Water Ditch Trail

A great place to run, ride, or walk the dog. The currently completed section crosses much of South Tacoma, and future construction will connect to the University of Washington downtown.
• cityoftacoma.org

Bob's Java Jive

A South Tacoma icon, the teapot-shaped building now offers beer and wine, live music and karaoke. Bar stools were taken from old school buses [with permission, we think]; the large primate in the glass cage has been outsourced.
• 2102 South Tacoma Way
• 253.475.9843
• bobsjavajive.com ❽

Porter's BBQ

Classic barbeque in large portions; salads and deserts. Porter's hot sauce is called "the Man." It is the region's only anthropomorphic condiment. Beer and wine.
• 5026 South Tacoma Way
• 253.383.7603
• porters-place.com ❾

Dawson's Bar & Grill

Spacious bar, reasonable prices. Live music several nights a week, no cover; pool and serious darts.
• 5443 South Tacoma Way
• 253.476.1421
• dawsonsbarandgrill.com ❿

B & I

The historic shopping center in the south end is now a very eclectic collection of shops. Arcade and merry-go-round for children of all ages. • 8012 South Tacoma Way
• 253.584.1672 ⓫

Patty's Burgers

Serves burgers and shakes in a '50s diner atmosphere. Big menu, large servings, reasonable prices. Not clear if there really is a Patty; we ask but they don't tell.
• 5615 South Tacoma Way
• 253.474.0844 ⓬

Star-Lite Swap & Shop

This former drive in theater now houses the Tacoma swap meet. Diverse customers and vendors. Items range from commonplace to hard to find. Caveat emptor.
• 8327 South Tacoma Way
• 253.588.8090 ⓭

Manitou Park

Manitou began as a camp ground on the edge of town, known for its large trees. An electric car line connecting Tacoma and Lakewood ran down the middle of the park. Electric cars are gone but there are now picnic areas, a sports complex, wading pool, and walking path.
• 4408 S American Lake Blvd. ⓮

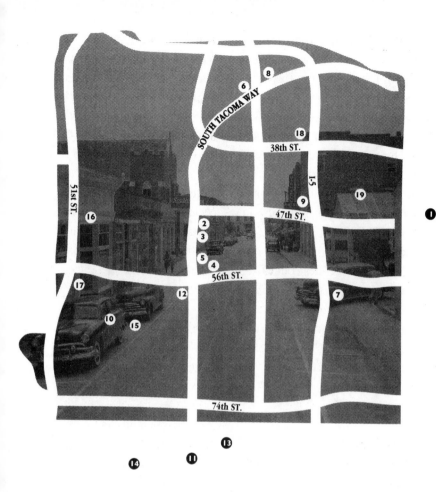

Meadow Park Golf Course

Quality public course at a reasonable price. 18-hole, executive 9-hole course, driving range, pro shop and restaurant. • 7108 Lakewood Dr. W • 253.473.3033 ⓯

Tacoma Firs Golf Center

A covered driving range, pro shop, putting and chipping greens and a small restaurant. Miniature golf available for children.
• 4504 S Tyler Street
• 253.472.6899.
• tacomafirsgolfcenter.com ⓰

Moctezuma's

Family-owned Mexican, actively involved in the community. Started in 1978 a few blocks away and moved to this spacious new place ten years later. Big menu. A second location in Gig Harbor. • 4102 S 56th St. • 253.474.5593
• moctezumas.com ⓱

Marlene's Market and Deli

Marlene's is one the pioneers in healthy food and living. This is the first of three locations in the area and has grocery [shelf goods, dairy and produce], extensive vitamins and food supplements, and a cafe. The staff is well-informed, not just about products but about upcoming events and community resources. • 2951 S 38th St.
• 253.472.4080
• marlenesmarket-deli.com **18**

Adriatic Grill

This is about loving what you do. Chef Bill Trudnowski has lived the food business from Army spoon to executive chef for a sprawling restaurant group. Now he's created a fine-tuned Italian place with beef, seafood (and vegetarian and gluten-free items by request). Craft cocktails, lots of special events, military discounts.
• 4201 S Steele St. • 253.475.6000
• adriaticgrill.com **19**

The Thea Foss Waterway

Slightly industrial with open park areas, condo complexes and the internationally famous Museum of Glass, the Foss Waterway is a destination area in the City of Destiny.

Alec Clayton

Thea's Park
This landscaped park features a 9/11 memorial, a 100-foot flag pole and a huge sculptural globe surrounded by a compass rose and "peace pole." The pole's inscription: "May peace prevail on Earth" in the 12 languages Of Tacoma's sister cities. • 405 Dock St. ❶

Foss Harbor Marina
Moorage or rental boats and kayaks for paddling around the waterway.

• 821 Dock St.
• 253.272.4404
• fossharbormarina.com ❷

The Foss Waterway Seaport
Boats, boats and more boats; classic boats, working boats and recreational boats on display and in the works with boat building and maintenance workshops and playful activities for kids.
• 705 Dock St. • 253.272.2750
• fosswaterwayseaport.org ❸

The Museum of Glass

The Museum is an international attraction. The hot shop looks like an ice cream cone turned upside-down and at 90 feet tall is one of Tacoma's most visible landmarks. Inside, the spacious galleries feature the work of renowned glass artists from all over the world. Stadium seats in the hot shop let visitors watch artisans blow glass. Kids [with grown-ups] are welcome in the Education Workshop, where they can learn about working with glass, hands-on. Docent-led and private tours [by appointment]. The gift shop is outstanding.
• 1801 Dock St. • 253.284.4750
• museumofglass.org ❹

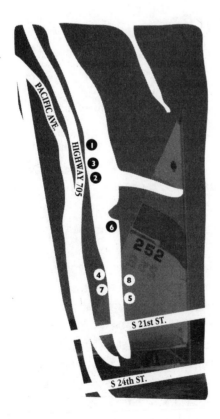

Evergreen Rowing

New and used shells for rowing and sculling; parts and equipment. An excellent resource for information on the local open water scene.
• 705 Dock St. • 360.357.6588 • evergreenrowing.com ❺

The Social Bar and Grill

An imaginative menu [snacks, entrees and desert], craft cocktails and an inviting patio.
• 1715 Dock St. • 253.301.3835
• thesocialbarandgrill.com ❻

Albers Brothers Mill

Ghosts of a storied industrial past still reside in the form of faded signs on the sides of this historic brick and timber building constructed in 1904. Next door to The Museum of Glass, it houses loft apartments and offices. • 1948 Dock St. ❼

Johnny's Dock

Facing The Museum of Glass from across the water, Johnny's Dock is one of Tacoma's oldest and most popular seafood and steak restaurants. Outdoor seating; marina.
• 1900 E D St. • 253.627.3186
• johnnysdock.com ❽

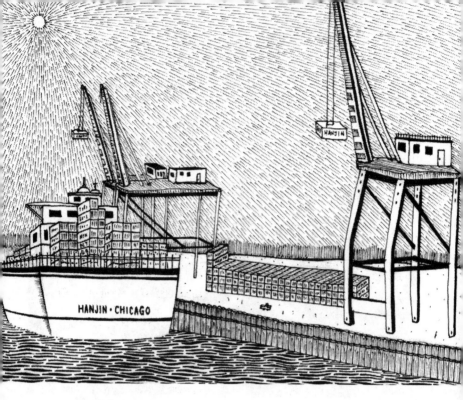

Port of Tacoma

The Port of Tacoma is an economic engine for the entire state, with activities connected to more than 43,000 family-wage jobs in Pierce County and 113,000 statewide. A strategic gateway to Asia and Alaska, the Port is a major center for containers, automobiles, heavy equipment, bulk and break-bulk cargoes. Port operations, wildlife and the water are accessible at the sites listed below. More information about public access at portoftacoma.com/public-access.

Tara Mattina

Observation Tower
Located in the parking lot of the Port of Tacoma Administration Building, this four-story platform provides panoramic views of the Sitcum Waterway, rail yards and marine terminals.
• 1 Sitcum Way ❶

Gog-le-hi-te Wetlands
This public overlook provides views of wetland habitat along the Puyallup River. The off-channel habitat supports a healthy ecosystem for juvenile salmon, plants and a variety of wildlife. The site is listed on Audubon Washington's Birding Trail Map to view herons, teal, kingfishers, gulls and sandpipers. • Lincoln Avenue and Stewart St. ❷

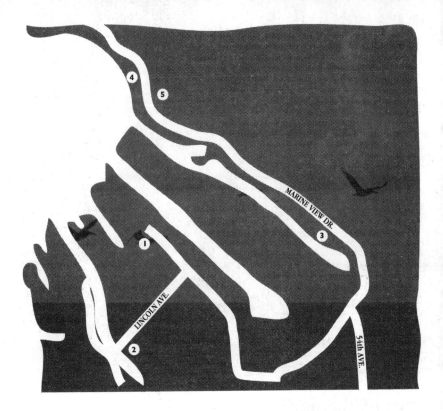

Place of Circling Waters

Most of this 30-acre site is fenced off to protect the habitat and wildlife, but a platform at the top of a paved walkway provides a picnic table with a view of Hylebos Creek, intertidal channels and forested open space. Salmon, kingfishers, hawks, herons and coyotes call this home.

• 1621 Marine View Dr. ❸

Dick Gilmur Shoreline Restoration and Kayak Launch

A wide gravel path leads from the planted bluff to the rocky beach, allowing car-top boats to launch from the shore. The site's restored shoreline provides habitat for the hundreds of birds and other wildlife that live along the storm-scoured shore. Native plants help anchor soil and provide shade, food and refuge. The parking area features pervious pavement to allow stormwater to filter into the ground rather than carry pollutants into the bay.

• 5002 Marine View Dr. ❹

Julia's Gulch

About 70 acres of steep forested open space provide rustic trails and a quiet spot to reconnect with nature. The site is listed on Audubon Washington's Birding Trail Map for viewing warblers, woodpeckers and bushtits.Just north of Viewpoint Park on Norpoint Way ❺

The Lincoln District

Tacoma's International District with services, retail and restaurants. South East Asian cuisine dominates; a smattering of Mexican eateries, an African American Soul Food Cafe' and American burger joints round out the neighborhood. There are three full-service grocery stores: East Asia Market; Hong Kong Supermarket; and Sien Thi Lucky Supermarket. Historic Lincoln High School sits at the corner of G and S. 37th Streets. Language barriers? Not when food is involved. Go. Enjoy. Write home about it.

Rosalind Bell

Uncle Thurm's

Uncle Thurm is a Soul Man, cooking up Classic Soul Food in his Soul Pots for the Souls of his Customers. And even people who enter without a soul... after sinking their teeth into his juicy, woosie, tender, crunchy catfish or chicken w/ greens cooked just right, or ribs or chitlins or mac 'n' cheese that will provoke a discussion on the road home...yeah, even if people don't have souls when they enter, Uncle Thurm will make sure they have 'em on the way out. Let the choir say, "Amen." Jazz Jam on Friday nights.

• 3709 S G St. • 253.475.1881 ❶

Tacqueria La Fondita

All taco trucks are not created equal. This one is above par... waaaay above par. Tortas. Burritos. Tacos. Enchiladas. Fresh. Sublime. Tasty. And healthy: omega 3s in the form of avocado slices with practically any order. It's a truck so people usually eat in the car or take it to go, though there's the lil makeshift dining area out front of the truck. The food will more than make up for no real seating.
- 3737 S G St.
- 253.472.2577 ❷

Lobster House

Hear Ye! Here Ye! Tacoma finally has a Chinese restaurant to write home about. Smack dab in the center of the Lincoln District sits this unassuming...ahem...non-descript gem. Dim Sum! a la carte is still Dim Sum! Shrimp w/ Chinese veggies (Bok Choy) so good folks smile like fools for days. Whole Crab w/ ginger sauce that cries out for sopping. • 711 S 38th St.
- 253.471.8982 ❸

Tho Tuong BBQ

Those crispy, shiny, whole ducks hanging in the window don't stay there long. A steady stream of mainly Vietnamese-speaking customers enter and down come the ducks, to be placed on the chopping block, boxed, w/wo the head, but always with pickled jalapeno and chef's special sauce, and sent on their way to some lucky person's dining table or desk. There's also roast pork, chicken feet, hog maws (soft and tender), Vietnamese coffee. Noodle Soup like no other. But the duck...must...try... the duck.
- 715 S 38th St.
- 253.474.2279 ❹

East Asia Market

This market has it: everything. Every market has seafood. Who has eel? They do. Every market has beef. Who has tongue? They do. Every market has fruit. Who has Durian? They do! Cookware. Food to go. Locally made tofu. It's like the United Nations of Food, this place; people and languages bumping up against one another from all over. Sake selection is large. Rice selection even larger. • 602 S 38th St.
- 253.473.3799 ❺

An-Hing Chinese Herbs and Grocery

Before there was Western Medicine there was this. Drawers and cupboards hold herbs and potions to cure whatever ails. Herbalists on hand to concoct herbs into a tea. There is also ginger candy that should come with an "addictive" warning. And some cures from other continents: African Sea Coconut, for one, a traditional herbal medicine for the relief of cough and chest congestion. Like leaving this century, this country.
- 767 S 38th St. • 253.474.3805 ❻

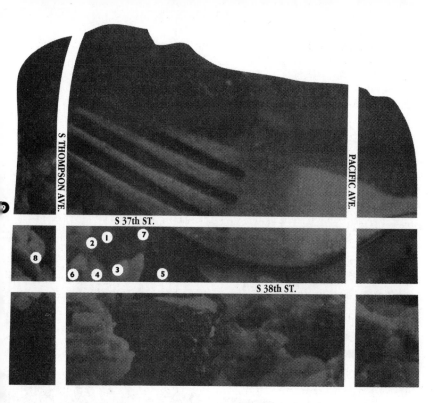

Lincoln Hardware

If this was a motorcycle club it would be Redwood Originals. Family owned and operated for more than 80 years. Vegetable seeds, suspenders, cast iron skillets, standard and obscure tools and supplies. Everybody needs something to carry.

3726 S G St.
- 253.472.1425
- lincolnhardware.net ❼

Lincoln Park

Just north of South 37th on Thompson, an active neighbor to Lincoln High School. The park is partly wooded, has picnic facilities, tennis and basketball courts and play equipment. ❽

Studio Moves Dance Center

Lessons for all ages in ballet, jazz and lyrical; private lessons and student performances.
- 3719 S M St.
- 253.212.9451 ❾
- studiomovesdancecenter.com

Hilltop

Once stigmatized because of drugs and gangs, in recent decades Tacoma's Hilltop has seen declining crime, an influx of young families and growing pride. Hilltop is a bustling district of restaurants, shops, and cultural facilities. Together, they create and sustain a diverse, thriving community.

Dawn Quinn

People's Park

A community hub, People's Park welcomes visitors with basketball courts, large grass plaza and amphitheater. Bob Henry's mural, "A Dream Coming True," is visible from the park and testament to Hilltop's multi-ethnic heritage.
• 9th St. and Martin Luther King Jr. Way ❶

Neighbors' Park

Sandwiched between S. J and I streets on S. 8th Neighbors' Park features a basketball court, newly renovated playground equipment, tetherball, picnic area and a popular community garden.
• S 8th & 'I' St. ❷

Quickie Too

Quickie Too is part of a Seattle-based family business started over 20 years ago. The Tacoma locale offers Southern soul food for vegetarians, vegans and the veg food-curious alike in the heart of Hilltop.
• 1324 Martin Luther King Jr. Way
• hillsidequickie.com ❸

Lele's

A neighborhood staple for 10 years, Lele's serves up Southeast Asian dishes such as curries, spring rolls, noodle salads, and Vietnamese pho in a tropically-decorated, cozy setting.
• 1012 Martin Luther King Jr. Way
• lelerestaurant.com ❹

Fulcrum

Fulcrum is one of Tacoma's great small galleries. Owner/artist Oliver Doriss infuses Hilltop pride in the space that also functions as a retail shop and artistic community hub. It's the place to be on Third Thursdays for the most innovative shows around.
• 1308 Martin Luther King Jr. Way
• 253.250.0520
• fulcrumtacoma.com ❺

Fabitat (Fab 5)

Fab 5 is an arts outreach organization that teaches area kids how to operate sound and video equipment, paint, rap, and express themselves. The Fabitat is their domain.
• 1316 Martin Luther King Jr. Way
• fab-five.org ❻

D.A.S.H. Center for the Arts

Primarily supporting inner-city youth without access to creative outlets, D.A.S.H. Center offers classes in dance, songwriting and recording, acting and more, and puts on events throughout the year.
• 1504 Martin Luther King Jr. Way
• thedashcenter.org ❼

1022 South

Heralded by cocktail fans and local and national media, 1022 South serves and creates inventive craft cocktails that favor the apothecary, as well as appetizers, plates and desserts made with local ingredients. • 1022 S J St. • 253.627.8588
• 1022south.com ❽

Tempest Lounge

Sleek, intimate and effortlessly cool, the Tempest is a welcome spot to all on the Hilltop, offering classic cocktails, beers, wine and a full dinner menu. Pleasant weather bonus: there are two patios for sunshine basking and people watching.
• 913 Martin Luther King Way
• 253.272.4904
• tempestlounge.com ❾

Guadalupe Land Trust Community Gardens

Functioning as an urban conservation non-profit, the Guadalupe Land Trust acquires and supports many Hilltop green spaces including the La Grande Community Garden and Hilltop House Garden, which neighbors use to grow fruits and vegetables for themselves or to donate to local charities. ❿
- 1106 Martin Luther King Jr. Way
- facebook.com/guadalupelandtrust

Grand Old Dames

On S. J Street lies a row of eight nearly identical Queen Anne style row houses. Nicknamed the "Grand Old Dames," the architecturally significant homes are historic landmarks and remain a testament to one of Tacoma's most prosperous historical periods.
- S J St. between S 7th and S 8th ⓫

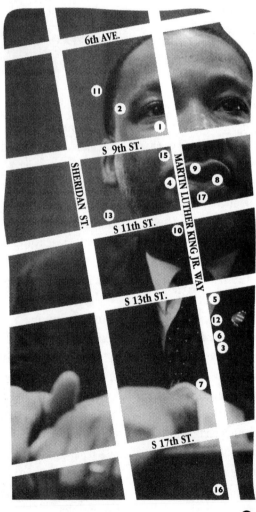

2nd Cycle Bike Collective

In 2008, four friends and avid bike riders conceived of the idea of a community bike shop. Today, it's a reality. The group aims to support, educate and advocate for cyclists in Hilltop and the Tacoma community.
• 1312 Martin Luther King Jr. Way
• 2ndcycle.org ⑫

Le Donut

Nestled on Hilltop, Le Donut is a curious sight amongst neighborhood homes, and the yellow building boasts donuts in large sizes. Offering the classics as well as trendier treats such as bacon maple bars, Le Donut is Tacoma's answer to Portland's Voodoo Doughnuts.
• 1317 S 11th St.
• 253.627.5877 ⑬

Papa Jones Barbecue

Ark/Tex barbecue from an established family of grillers and smokers. Generous servings, lots of napkins.
• 1902 Martin Luther King Way
• 253.572.2513 ⑭

Johnson Candy Company

A boutique candy factory and retailer, in this location since 1949. Hand-made chocolates and classic truffles.
• 924 Martin Luther King Way
• 253.272.8504 ⑮

MLK Ballet

A tuition-free dance program for area kids. Led by professional dancers, the program works in a restored church and is an important node in the area dance scene, with student performances and professional benefits. • 253.906.2190
• mlkballet.blog.com

The Fish House

Definitely a neighborhood place and not putting on any airs, the Fish House serves catfish sandwiches, Philly steaks, hot wings and more.
• 1814 Martin Luther King Jr. Way
• 253.383.7144 ⑯

Peterson Bros. 1111

The most recent addition to the Hill's nightlife circuit, the glitz-free 1111 offers standard drinks and tasty pub fare. A much-needed neighborhood bar in Hilltop.
• 1111 S 11th St. ⑰

University District

Set in century-old brick buildings on the hillside overlooking Union Station, the Port and Mount Rainier, the University of Washington is becoming a force in Tacoma's economic and cultural development. The streets around the campus are vibrant and graduates play an increasingly important role in business and in civic life. 1900 Commerce Street, 253.692.4000, tacoma.uw.edu

Courtenay Chamberlin

University Bookstore
The U bookstore has a strong general readers' section, university gear and art supplies as well as textbooks.
- 1754 Pacific
- 253.692.4440
- washington.edu ❶

Tacoma Art Museum
Dedicated to Northwest art since 1935, the Museum also features national and international touring exhibits. The current building, designed by Antoine Predock and opened in 2003, has 12,000 square feet of gallery space and about

8,000 square feet dedicated to arts education. Gift shop and cafe on site, as well as space indoors and outside for contemplation. As we go to press, the Museum announced two significant gifts. One will double gallery space to almost 30,000 square feet; the other brings 280 pieces of Western American art from Helga and Erivan Haub. The Haubs' gift is considered one of the leading such collections in the world.
• 1701 Pacific
• 253.272.4258
• tacomaartmuseum.org ❷

Chihuly Glass Walking Tours

Tacoma Art Museum docents lead tours in and outside the museum about the art and career of Tacoma native and internationally renowned glass artist, Dale Chihuly. Call for schedule.
• 1701 Pacific
• 253.272.4258
• tacomaartmuseum.org

Ear for Art: Chihuly Glass Cell Phone Tour

A narrator, and Chihuly himself, talk about his installations at Tacoma Art Museum, Union Station, Bridge of Glass, UWT Library, and The Swiss Pub. Free. • 888.411.4220
• tacomaartmuseum.org

Bridge of Glass

A 500-foot pedestrian walkway connects the U District to the Museum of Glass and Foss Waterway. The Bridge features three Chihuly installations: Seaform Pavilion, Crystal Towers and Venetian Wall.
• 1901 Pacific ❸

Washington State History Museum

Interactive exhibits, historic artifacts and kids' History Lab tell stories of people, places, and industries that shaped the state, from Native Americans to present day. Permanent exhibits include model railroading and the Hall of Washington History. The Museum, opened in 1996, spans over 100,000 square feet and includes a theater, gift shop and rental spaces. • 1911 Pacific
• 888.238.4373
• wshs.org ❹

Children's Museum of Tacoma

An art studio and playscapes that mimic woods, waterfall and vessel with an emphasis on unstructured play and imagination. Kids (and some adults) explore, splash, pretend, create and build. Available for parties. Pay-as-You-Will admission reduces the risk the kids won't like it. Not much risk. Cafe Play in partnership with Satellite Coffee.
• 1501 Pacific
• 253.627.6031
• playtacoma.org ❺

Union Station

Built in 1911 as a rail station and now a federal courthouse, the Station is one of the preservation movement's early victories.

The rotunda features five Chihuly installations; the bronze traveler on the sidewalk welcomes newcomers. Free, open weekdays.
• 1717 Pacific ❻

Tollefson Square
A triangular 'square' with water feature, wide terraced stair steps and a towering cedar Welcome Figure. The Square hosts events from ice skating to art festivals. Food carts some days. • Pacific and S 17th St. ❼

Anthem Coffee and Tea
Warm friendly space, local roasts, good breakfast and lunch. The theme is "live loud" and the staff keeps the place lively. Dillano-roasted coffee. • 1911 Pacific • Anthemcoffeeandtea.com [also in Puyallup at 210 W. Pioneer] ❽

Prairie Line Trail
In 1873 this half-mile corridor was designated as the Northern Pacific Railroad's western terminus. Legend has it Tacoma, Seattle and Walla Walla, competing for leadership of the Washington Territory, each selected an element on which to build. Walla Walla chose the state penitentiary, Seattle the University of Washington and Tacoma the railroad terminus. Tacoma's choice looked very smart - until the terminus was moved north. The planned trail is somewhat overgrown at this writing. Look for temporary and permanent art installations.
• 1900 Commerce St.
• tacomaculture.org ❾

Art and Architecture Walking Tour
Even though the web site is labeled "Campus Walking Tour," it's a comprehensive guide to the art and architecture of the area.
• tacoma.washington.edu

Glass Blowing Classes and Demonstrations
Two locations for viewing artists at work and for blowing glass. Classes, birthday parties, team skill building workshops, special events. Check schedules online.
M-Space Glass Arts
• 2310 S Holgate St. • 253.779.0101
• mspacetacoma.com
Tacoma Glassblowing Studio
• 114 S 23rd St. • 253.383.3499
• tacomaglassblowing.com ❿

Harmon Brewery and Eatery

Hearty Northwest pub food and five Harmon-brewed ales on tap in this historic, refurbished brick furniture manufacturing plant. Parmesan garlic fries are a stand-out. Spacious interior and a big menu. Family friendly.
- 1938 Pacific
- 253.383.2739
- harmonbrewingco.com ❶

Pacific Grill

Exposed beam ceilings and brick walls of the historic Waddell Building combine with intimate lighting, curvaceous bar and upscale fare with NW flare. Dinner menu is strong on Pacific seafood but offers steaks too. Box lunches and private dining room available. Happy hour all day! At least while they're open.
- 1502 Pacific
- 253.627.3535
- pacificgrilltacoma.com ❷

The Swiss Pub

The Swiss Society opened its Hall in 1913, in an era when immigrants clustered around memories of home. Now the Swiss is a one-of-a-kind pub serving salads, sandwiches, seafood, soups, cocktails, wines and an impressive selection on tap. Live music, pool tables. Great glass art over the bar. Kids' menu until evening becomes night.
- 1904 Jefferson
- 253.572.2821
- theswisspub.com ❸

Metro Coffee

Traditional coffeehouse nestled on UWT stairs; features locally roasted Lighthouse Coffee, artisanal pastries and artificial-hormone-free milk. • 1901 Jefferson, Suite B
- 253.627.8152 ❹

Two Koi

Fusion and traditional Japanese dining in booths overlooking Tollefson Plaza. Private dining rooms and sushi bar seating with view of the open style kitchen. • 1552 Commerce St. #100 • twokoi.com ❺

Indochine

Exposed brick, dark cherry, iron, and rich draperies set the tone for Thai cuisine with Asian and Indian influences. Best orange chicken ever. Probably. Check out the bar's color-shifting wall. • 1924 Pacific
- 253.272.8200
- indochinedowntown.com ❻

Tacoma City Grocer IGA

Since it caters to downtown dwellers and office workers, City Grocer emphasizes staples, fresh fruit and snacks to stash in the hotel room and lots of grab-and-go meals. • Pacific Plaza, 1250 Pacific
- 253.830.5755
- citygroceriga.com ❼

Greater Tacoma Convention and Trade Center

An unusual setting for northwest art. Among the highlights: the bathroom stall tiles. Stunning views from the top floor.
• 1500 Broadway • 253.830.6601
• tacomaconventioncenter.com ⑱

Hotel Murano

A world-class glass art collection extends from the lobby through the guest floors. Comfortable, modern rooms have views of downtown, the foothills and Mt. Rainier. Visitors are welcome to explore the public spaces. The lobby staff is distinctively good. • 320 Broadway
• 253.238.8000
• hotelmurano- tacoma.com ⑲

Bite

The hotel's art-filled setting extends to dining, with local seasonal offerings for breakfast, lunch and dinner. A nicely varied menu with vegetarian options; good privacy in the booths; a private room is available. Hotel Murano 4th Floor, 1320 Broadway • 253.238-8000
• hotelmuranotacoma.com ⑳

Savi Day Spa

Located within Hotel Murano, Savi offers body pampering services including facials, massages, manicures and pedicures.
• 1320 Broadway
• 253.274.8999
• savidayspa.com ㉑

Urban XChange

Eclectic vintage and modern recycled clothing and accessories for men and women. Buy, sell, and trade on a walk-in basis.
• 1932 Pacific
• 253.572.2280
• etsy.com/shop/urbanxchange ㉒

Bleach

Men's and women's clothing that looks like a hard-knock life. Skateboards are involved. Brands include Brixton, Loser Machine and our favorite, Vestal.
• 1934 Pacific • 253.292.1694
• bleachlife.com ㉓

South Sound Running

For the perfect fit on running or walking shoes. Employees are runners and can offer recommendations on routes, races and equipment. It's more about kinesthesiology here and less about selling.
• 1736 Pacific • 253. 593.8786
• southsoundrunning.com ㉔

Vertical World Climbing Gym

An indoor option for youth and adults. In case it's cloudy. Day passes, punch cards, and gear rentals. • 102 S 24th St.
• 253.683.4791
• verticalworld.com ㉕

Native Quest Cafe and Bookstore

A lovingly-created space featuring traditional and new Native foods, and crafts and art by Native artisans. The bookstore carries over 5,500 titles, the entire inventory of Macrae's Indian Books. Workshops and events.

• 2354 Jefferson • 253. 627.8033
• nativequest.net ㉖

T Town Apparel

This custom screen print and embroidery business has a small storefront specializing in Tacoma gear, from 253 heart decals to graphic tees and sweatshirts. It's the mother ship for gritty Tacoma pride.

• 1934 Market • 253.472.2960
• ttownapparelonline.com ㉗

Embellish

A most thoughtful salon, with services for men and children. This is not, "gimme number two, Lou;" the staff is focused on hair and scalp health in a relaxing, renewing environment.

1121 Court D 253.752.8144 Embellishtacoma.com ㉘

THE ELEPHANTS 7/2
BEL BIV BEVOE 7/3
MLK BALLET 7/4

Theater District

Anchored by three landmark theaters and home to Tacoma's leading performing arts organizations, the Theater District grows ever more vibrant year by year. In these few square blocks are opportunities to eat well and adventurously, appreciate historic architecture, poke through shops on Antique Row. There's lots of public art – permanent and done on the fly by guerilla artists. And when the spring begins the city's original farmers market springs to life. This is the heart of downtown, where art and living are intertwined.

Rebecca Young

The Pantages

Built in 1918 and modeled after the theater at Versailles, the Pantages is home to the Tacoma Symphony and Tacoma Opera and has hosted performers from Wanda Sykes to Ira Glass. This is one of only five theaters remaining from the empire of Alexander Pantages, a Greek immigrant who amassed a chain of over 70 facilities across North America. Five years of renovation [1978-83] sparked the revival of downtown. Like the Rialto [below] the Pantages is on the National Register of Historic Places.
• 901 Broadway • 253.591.5890
• broadwaycenter.org ❶

Theater on the Square

The newest of Broadway Center for the Performing Arts' theater trio, contemporary TOTS is used for more intimate performances. Not a bad seat among the 300.
•901 Broadway •253.591.5890
•broadwaycenter.org ❷

Theater Square

A favorite lunch spot on sunny or almost sunny days, the Square features a dancing fountain, a salmon made of recycled aluminum cans and an imposing trompe-l'oeil mural. •Between 9th and 11th on Broadway ❸

Broadway Farmers Market

The street's hopping on Thursdays for the city's biggest, oldest market. Heavy to produce and handcrafted foods, flowers and lunches.
•S 9th and Broadway
•10 a.m.-3p.m., Thursdays May through October

Pythian Temple

Built in 1906 by architect Frederick Heath for the Commencement Lodge Number 7 of the Knights of Pythias, which is still active with about 50 members. This is an architectural and historic treasure, restored in the 1990s. Though open only to members most of the time, the Temple hosts infrequent musical performances and historic tours, and – time permitting – can arrange for a member to show the facilities to guests. The organization can be reached by mail at Chancellor Commander, Knights of Pythias Commencement Lodge #7 Tacoma, WA 98402; the Temple is located at 926 Broadway ❹

Sundance Cafe

Fast and friendly. The roast beef melt and Sundance Special get good marks.
•950 Broadway •253.572.9583 ❺

LeRoy Jewelers

A downtown institution since 1941. Steph Farber and Phyllis Harrison carry ready-made pieces but love helping people "tell their stories" through custom jewelry. Steph was recently recognized by the American Gem Trade Association for his innovation in design. This is where art meets the precious but inert.
• 940 Broadway • 253.272.3377
• leroyjewelers.com ❻

The Art Stop

A gallery within LeRoy Jewelers specializes in contemporary crafts with a focus on pottery and Judaica.
• 940 Broadway • 253.274.1630
• artstoptacoma.com ❼

Woolworth Building

The windows of the vacant Woolworth store have been turned into a gallery by Spaceworks Tacoma, a project designed to fill empty storefronts with art.
• 955 Broadway ❽
spaceworkstacoma.wordpress.com

Tollbooth Gallery

Outside the Woolworth building is the world's smallest gallery. The once-abandoned TV-Tacoma information booth is dedicated to experimental video and fine arts.
• 9th and Broadway ❾

Masks

This large collection of stone and metal masks was created by artist Doug Granum. Hung throughout the Theater District on walls and light poles. (Granum also did the big stone pieces in front of the Pantages.)
• douglasgranum.com

Varsity Grill

The space is huge. Kids eat free. Wednesdays after 4, steak for $3. Friday-Saturday, live music. Karaoke from 8 till closing (all ages until 10:30).
• 1114 Broadway • 253.627.1229
• varsitygrill.com ❿

Galanga Thai

Named after a gingery root, this busy restaurant focuses on the spices, herbs and fresh ingredients of Southeast Asia. • 1129 Broadway
• 253.272.3393
• galangathai.com ⓫

Mad Hat: A Tea Company

A romantic spot, great with a book or friend – and a cup of hot or iced tea from an exotic menu. Tea and accessories for sale and art and CDs by local folks. • 1130 Commerce & 1127 Broadway (Two entrances)
• 253.441.2111
• madhattea.com ⓬

Fujiya Japanese Restaurant

Opened in 1984, Fujiya offers fresh sushi and full Japanese menu. Chefs can be watched from seats at the bar. • 1125 Court C
• 253.627.5319
• fujiyatacoma.com ⓭

Fountain

It looks like a giant stack of children's blocks and on a sunny day this fountain becomes a child magnet, fun for climbing and foot dipping. • 11th and Broadway

The Rialto

Also built in 1918, Broadway Center's Rialto was once part of a national movie chain. In mid-December, home of Puget Sound Revels, a regular in the Rialto's line-up. • 910 Court C • 253.591.5890
• broadwaycenter.org ⓮

Mural on the back of the Rialto

Initiated by Urban Grace and funded by a neighborhood grant, an exuberant mural by graffiti artist group Fab 5 brightens the block.
• S 9th and Market

Urban Grace: The Downtown Church

Urban Grace, housed in a 1924 Gothic Revival style building, is an interdenominational church known for civil rights events and sponsorship of a poet laureate program and poetry series. • 902 Market
• 253.272.2184
• urbangracetacoma.org ⓯

Tacoma Comedy Club

Nationally touring comics Thursdays through Sundays; free open-mic night on Wednesdays. Free nights for college students, ladies and troops.
• 933 Market
• 253.282.7203
• tacoma-comedyclub.com ⓰

Bostwick Tully's

Yeah it's a chain, but it's in the wedge-shaped 1887 Bostwick Building. And it was Kevin Kline's pizzeria in I Love You to Death. There's a piano, a private meeting room – and good coffee.
• 764 Broadway
• 253.627.5646
• tullyscoffeeshops.com

Antique Row

Broadway from South 9th to South 7th is lined with antique shops – including Sanford and Son, boasting "30 dealers on three floors" and Lily Pad Antiques & Old Toys. ⓱

A Little Touch of Magick

Gift for the Goth woman? This is the place. Clothing, jewelry and other finery. • 763 Broadway
• 253.272.0744
• alittletouchofmagick.com ⓲

Glenna's Clothing

Upscale vintage women's clothing. One shopper says this is "the place to go to look like Jackie O." Could be true and it rhymes.
• 783 Broadway • 253.627.8501 ⓳

Broadway Garages

Urban artists from all over the state gather every Sunday to repaint the walls of this garage through a business/city/art partnership. Other days? People park their cars. • 723 Broadway ⓴

Frost Park Chalk Off

Named for fallen cop Larry Frost, this tiny park was once doomed to be fenced off. But since 2008, it's been the scene of Friday chalk art challenges. • 9th and Pacific
• 12 p.m. to 1 pm., Fridays; spring to early autumn ㉑

Over the Moon Cafe

For a theater date or anniversary dinner, Over the Moon radiates romance. The food – Northwest and European – is delicious, too. Lunch and dinner.
• 709 Opera Alley (Court C)
• 253.284.3722
• overthemooncafe.net ㉒

Fibers Etc.

This tiny shop and studio is filled floor to ceiling with high-end yarn, needles and other supplies. Open afternoons four days a week.
• 705 Opera Alley (Court C)
• 253.572.1859 ㉓

Puget Sound Pizza

Great pizza in unassuming surroundings; breakfast on weekends, full bar with karaoke. PSP's a popular spot. • 317 S 7th St.
• 253.383.4777 ㉔

The Mix

The Mix calls itself Tacoma's "favorite gay bar, straight bar, everyone bar." Visit for friendly bartenders and friendlier patrons. Cheap drinks, karaoke and billiards.
•635 St. Helens •253.383.4327
• themixtacoma.com ㉕

Tacoma Metal Arts Center

TMAC offers instruction in jewelry making and metal arts. A fully equipped studio is available for rental after students have taken at least one class. •711 St. Helens #102 •253.227.1694
• tacomametalarts.com

Guitar Maniacs

Vintage guitars, amplifiers, drums and accessories bought, sold and traded by people who know their stuff. •737 St. Helens
•253.272.4741
• guitarmaniacs.com ㉖

Club Silverstone

Nothing says Saturday night like dancing under double disco balls. Every holiday is an excuse for a party. •739 St. Helens •253.404.0273
• clubsilverstone.com ㉗

Rainbow Center

At this LGBT community center, people use the Internet, check out books, play pool, watch a movie and talk to supportive listeners. Information, resources, advocacy.
•741 St. Helens ㉘
•253.383.2318 • rainbowcntr.org

AmeRAWcan Bistro

Raw food is the draw at AmeRAWcan (pronounced American) Bistro. Breakfast porridge? Pureed pecans. Chips? Kale. Fettuccini? Zucchini. Order off the table's iPad.
•745 St. Helens
•253.327.1962 ㉙

Deltan Club

Bar and restaurant across from the Theater District Light Rail stop features live drag shows and dancing. All orientations welcome.
•733 Commerce
•253.680.9328 ㉚

Poledello

Pole dance instruction in a brick-walled studio. Group and private instruction. Pole fitness parties.
•715 Commerce •253.509.8811
• poledello.com ㉛

Dorky's Arcade

Packed with old-school video games and pinball machines, 25 or 50 cents each. Food and beer. No minors after 9.
•754 Pacific
•253.627.4156
• facebook.com/dorkys253 ㉜

Paddy Coyne's Irish Pub

Soda bread and Irish stew washed down with a Smithwicks by the blazing fire. That's a chilly evening at Paddy Coyne's.
•815 Pacific
•253.272.6963
• paddycoynes.net ㉝

The Office

The Office features American pub-style food and a 2-5-3 happy hour ($2, $5 and $3 items). Tater tot nachos, HD sports, courtyard, jukebox. • 813 Pacific • 253.572.3222 • theofficeonpacific.com **34**

Learning Sprout

Two floors of fun. Once just a teacher supply store, Learning Sprouts now offers a wealth of educational and imagination-igniting toys, games, puzzles, books, art supplies and more. Events, too. • 809 Pacific • 253.274.0136 • learningsprout.com **35**

Meconi's Pub & Eatery

Another beloved hangout, Meconi's is in one of the city's most historic blocks. Hearty pub food, trivia nights, bingo, HD sports, WiFi. • 709 Pacific • 253.383.3388 • tacomapub.com **36**

Pho 701 Bistro and Bar

Vietnamese pho, fresh spring rolls, mango and papaya salads, chicken satay, beer and wine . • 701 Pacific • 253.627.9225 • pho701bistrobar.com **37**

Elks Temple Building

Designed in 1915 by architect Edouard Frere Champney, the unoccupied beauty is slated for restoration by the McMenamin Bros. to hold a hotel, spa, and restaurant. • S 7th St. and Commerce **38**

Spanish Steps

Adjacent to the Elks building, the steps were also built in 1915. They were patterned after the Spanish Steps in Rome and are among the most endangered historic resources in Washington. **39**

Old City Hall

Another Tacoma fixture, the 1893 Italiante clock tower of Old City Hall looks out on Commencement Bay. Sadly, the building is flood-damaged inside, its fate debated. • 625 Commerce • thestratfordcompany.com **40**

Stink

"The new aroma of Tacoma" is this deli's playful catch phrase. Artisan and imported cheeses, cured meats, crusty bread, soup, salad, wine, beer. • 628 St. Helens • 253.426.1347 • stinktacoma.com **41**

Amocat Cafe

A popular spot that features coffee, tea from Mad Hat, pastry, salads, grilled paninis, beer, wine. Tacoma gifts, local artists, free WiFi. • 625 St. Helens • 253.242.3370 • amocatcafe.com **42**

Goddess of Commerce

She replaces an 1885 Goddess of Commerce statue that came down in 1950. The new Goddess wears symbols of Tacoma's industries and city buildings. • S Baker and St. Helens

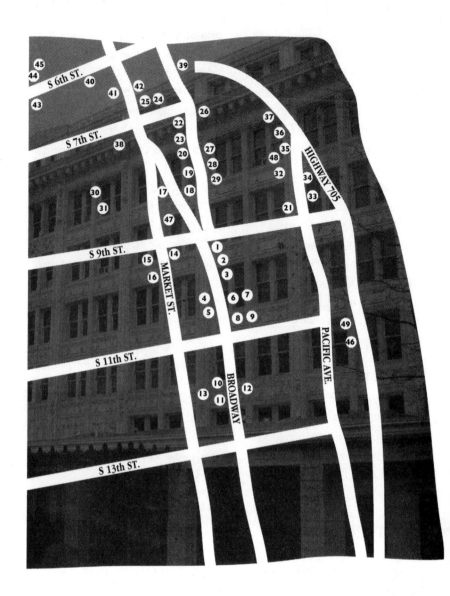

The Grand Cinema

Best popcorn in town, plus independent, documentary and foreign films not available closer than Seattle, the nonprofit art-house theater is a Tacoma institution. Memberships available.

- 606 S. Fawcett St.
- 253.593.4474
- www.grandcinema.com ❹❸

38

Corina Bakery

Snuggled next to The Grand, Corina's new digs make it ideal to pair with a movie date. Scones, quiche, muffins, bread, more. It's all from scratch. Wedding and other special items by order. • 602 S. Fawcett
• 253-627-5070
• www.corinabakery.com ❹❹

Infinite Soups

Tiny spot serving dozens of fresh homemade soups with a menu that changes daily. Like Seinfeld's Soup Nazi only the people are nice. Tasting cups. Creamy, noncreamy; vegan and vegetarian options. Bread from Corina Bakery. Take-out only. • 445 Tacoma Ave. S
• 253.274.0232
• infinitesoups.com ❹❺

Watermark Gifts

When downtown was emptied out in the 1970s, LeRoy's stayed and Watermark stepped in. A large, tasteful and varied collection of gifts and cards, soaps and oils - and the nicely odd. The kind of place that has a proprietor, and she's a good one. • 1115 A • 253.383.2041
• watermarkgifts.com ❹❻

Margaret's Cafe

Looking in it's nothing special but that's an illusion. Margaret Erwin is one of the best food people in town and serves a changing menu of small-batch soups and sandwiches and super desserts. • 754 St. Helens
• 253.274.8788 ❹❼

The Rhodes Medical Arts Building

Now city hall; the lobbies and stairways are glorious examples of Art Deco. • 747 Market

Ledger Square and Ben Gilbert Park

At the intersection of Market, St. Helens and South 7th, honors an early Tacoma newspaper (the Daily Ledger) and an esteemed newsman. A small, refreshing spot.

Matador

Imaginative updated TexMex (nothing says El Paso like blackened Ahi) and a gluten-free menu; craft cocktails, dessert, cool environment. Busy with business lunch and after-work drinks.
• 721 Pacific • 253.627.7100
• matadorrestaurants.com ❹❽

Murray Morgan Bridge

Crossing the Foss Waterway at South 11th Street, the bridge is named for the pre-eminent northwest historian of his generation – and a former bridge tender who wrote when things were slow. Built in 1913, it's under renovation but open to pedestrians and cyclists. ❹❾

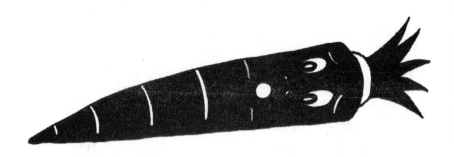

Vegan-friendly Tacoma restaurants
By Dawn Quinn, *Blogger at VeganMoxie.com*

Tacoma has dozens of cruelty-free and delicious options that entice even meat eaters to return. No matter the craving, this list has something for everyone.

Quickie Too
The first and only all-vegan restaurant in Tacoma; serves up rich comfort food that brings the carnivores back for more; lunch, dinner and weekend brunch. •1324 Martin Luther King Jr. Way •hillsidequickie.com

Caffe Dei
All-vegetarian coffee shop and cafe; fantastic espresso and tea drinks as well as locally made gluten-free vegan baked goods, raw meals, juices and sandwiches. •2607 6th Avenue •253.572.2550

Amerawcan Bistro
Downtown; eating fresh salads, raw/living dishes and other wholesome foods and drinks made convenient for residents and visitors.
•745 St Helens Ave. •amerawcanbistro.com

Gateway to India
One of the first restaurants in town to label their items "vegetarian" or "vegan;" earns extra points for offering solid vegan dishes for dinner and in their unbeatable lunch buffet seven days a week. •2603 6th Ave.
•gatewaytoindiarestaurant.com

Peanut Sauce Thai
Near Tacoma Mall; dedicates a good section of their menu entirely to vegetarian dishes. Anything on the veg menu can be made vegan on request. Great for parties and casual meals. •5003 Tacoma Mall Blvd.
•peanutsaucethaicuisine.com

El Toro

Five locations including Lakewood and Parkland; authentic, fresh vegan Mexican food becomes convenient. Try the vegetarian fajitas or burritos, and specify vegan. • eltorofamily.com

Silk Thai

These folks understand the vegan diet and easily make their much-loved curries, soups and noodle dishes without fish sauce or any non-veg ingredients. Ambiance is perfect for a date or special occasion.
• 3401 6th Ave. • silkthaicafe.com

Marlene's Market & Deli

With a fresh juice, soup and salad bar and sandwiches made in-house (not to mention the entire natural foods store that surrounds) this is the perfect vegan-friendly lunch spot. • 2951 S 38th St. • marlenesmarket-deli.com

Corina Bakery

Vegans need sweet treats, too. Molly Ott and crew get it; they offer up vegan and gluten-free cakes, cookies, and more to accompany excellent coffee and tea every day. • 602 S Fawcett Ave. • corinabakery.com

Pho V&V

Hearty, flavorful vegetarian broth accompanies tofu, vegetables and rice noodles in vegan-ized bowls of pho. Add a side of tofu spring rolls for the perfect lunch or dinner. • 5434 South Tacoma Way • phovandv.com

Infinite Soups

Daily vegetarian and vegan options posted in the shop and online; always at least four of each, making eating healthy in the Stadium district easy and delicious. • 445 Tacoma Ave. • infinitesoups.com

Indochine

For a fancy vegan dinner downtown; a pan-Asian melange of cuisines with seasonal vegetables; all dishes to order, so vegan is easy. • 1924 Pacific Ave.
• indochinedowntown.com

1022 South

Cocktails [olives, onions and cherries are vegan, right?] and enticing fare; small and large plates, inventive craft cocktails. • 1022 S J St.
• 1022south.com

Stadium District

Named for its iconic public high school, this is one of the South Sound's most vibrant neighborhoods, with stunning views of Commencement Bay, lively restaurants and bars, parks and century-old architecture. Many residents meet their everyday needs without driving; visitors can walk the day and into the evening.

John Idstrom

No visit to the District is complete without a stroll around **Stadium High School**, built in 1906 as a railroad hotel and renovated in 2006. [When school is in session please check in at the office.] Perched on the edge of a bluff overlooking Commencement Bay, Stadium was featured in Touchstone Pictures' Ten Things I Hate About You, starring Heath Ledger; Stadium Bowl was voted by ESPN as one of the top ten high school football venues in the U.S.. Carved into a deep

gulch, the Bowl seats 15,000 spectators; the open end offers expansive northerly views of Puget Sound and Browns Point. The Bowl has hosted notable speakers including presidents Teddy Roosevelt, Wilson and Harding. Running the stairs is a common – and vigorous – workout. • 111 N E St.
• 253.571.3100 ❶

Maxwell's Restaurant
In the historic Walker Building. Art deco elegance without being stuffy. Handcrafted cocktails, local/seasonal entrees and small plates. Extensive bar menu for more casual diners • 454 St. Helens
• 253.683.4115
• maxwell's-tacoma.com ❷

Doyle's Public House
For futbol/football/soccer, this is the bar. Games broadcast live whenever possible on several big screen TVs. Irish suds star here but there's a brew for any palate. Food approaches gastropub status. Open early for key matches.
• 208 St. Helens • 253.272.7468
• doylespublichouse.com ❸

Kings Books
The South Sound's Powell's. New, used, rare, out-of-print and more. Great section on Tacoma/South Sound history; special events; cats.
• 218 St. Helens
• 253.627.5070
• kingsbookstore.com ❹

The Hob Nob
No-nonsense American fare and political power breakfasts at this homey site across from Wright Park. Breakfasts feature omelets, waffles, hotcakes and (notably) corned beef hash with poached eggs. A crowd scene on Sunday mornings.
• 716 6th Ave. • 253.272.3200
• hobnobtacoma.com ❺

Tacoma Wine Merchant/ Enoteca
A back-to-basics wine boutique; owner/operator Bill Bonnie's specialty is sourcing excellent, lesser-known wines in the $10-15 range, weighted toward European labels. Informal wine bar with by-the-glass selections, cheese platters and home-made artisanal nibbles.
• 21 Tacoma Ave. N • 253.779.8258
• tacomawinemerchants.com ❻

Harmon Hub
A lively brewpub; food's a cut above. Pizza, pasta, burgers, salads etc. This is the sister to the original Harmon location near UW Tacoma. Breakfast served weekends.
• 203 Tacoma Ave. S
• 253.683.4606
• hub.harmonbrewingco.com ❼

Harvester
Plain Jane food served quick and easy. Open daily for breakfast, lunch and dinner.
• 298 Tacoma Ave. N
• harvestertacoma.com ❽

Frisko Freeze

A local legend , known for the vintage drive-in look as well as good food. Frisko Freeze puts the grease in greasy spoon. Cheeseburgers and fries. The blackberry shake is a Northwest Classic.

- 1201 Division
- 253.272.6843
- friskofreeze.com **9**

Parkway Tavern

Beer stars here, with some rare finds. Good pub food including burgers, sandwiches and salads. Nothing deep-fried. The clientele is mostly neighborhoodies. Service is knowledgeable and attentive.

- 313 N I St. • 253.383.8748
- parkwaytavern.com **10**

Stadium Thriftway

Recently renovated; includes an expansive deli/sandwich/to-go section and excellent wine shop. Great for picking up a picnic to take to Wright Park.

- 618 N 1st St.
- 253.627.8275
- stadiumthriftway.com **11**

Francos

A real Italian tailor, from hems to handmade suits. In addition to tailoring, this men's shop features a well-chosen selection of mostly imported, upscale shirts, sweaters, ties, etc.
- 16 Tacoma Ave. N
- 253.627.2336 ⓬

Ball Auto

Old school service station, now in its third generation of ownership.
- 116 Tacoma Ave. N
- 253.272.3562 ⓭

Ranko's Drug

Throwback family-owned drugstore, resembling big box franchises not in the least. Post Office in the back.
- 101 Tacoma Ave. N
- 253.383.2411 ⓮

1st Presbyterian Church

Built in 1925, this church is an excellent example of Romanesque architecture, designed by famous church architect Ralph Adams Cram. • 20 Tacoma Ave. S
- fpctacoma.com ⓯

Residences

The neighborhood boasts many well-preserved homes from the late 1890's. The North Slope Historic District was created to recognize their significance. Many buildings can be found on the tree-lined North Yakima Avenue or in the area immediately north of Tacoma Ave. • tacomanorthslope.com

Wright Park

The District gets its name from the high school but its heart and soul is Wright Park. With a perimeter of almost exactly a mile, this 20 acre gem has walking trails, duck pond, mature native trees, public art and a lawn bowling green. Updates completed in 2004 include a re-designed children's playground with state-of-the art equipment.
- 501 S I St. ⓰

Seymour Conservatory

Voted Best Place to Relax in Tacoma and listed on the National Historic Register. This all-glass conservatory features hundreds of exotic tropical plants and a small gift shop. Open Tues.- Sun., 10:30 a.m.-4:00 p.m.
- 316 S. G St. (inside Wright Park).

Annie Wright School

Over 100 years old, with one of the few girls' boarding departments on the west coast. A terrific blend of old and new architecture.
- 827 Tacoma Ave. N
- 253.272.2216 • aw.org ⓱

Garfield Park

Expansive playing fields and a large, popular children's playground are the main attractions of this pleas-ant, quiet park.
- 400 N Borough Rd. ⓲

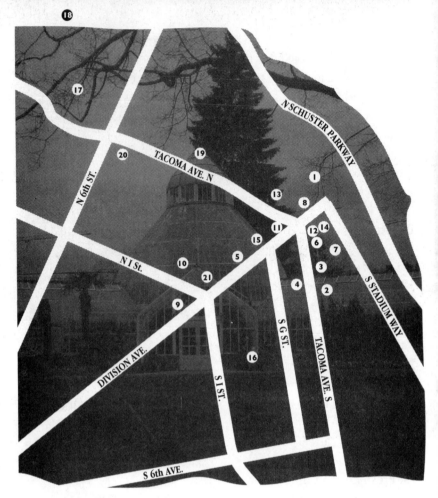

Chinaberry Hill

1889 Grand Victorian and adjoining cottage with luxury accommodations. • 302 Tacoma Ave. N
• 253.272.1282
• chinaberryhill.com ⓲

The Villa

Grand Mediterranean villa furnished in Italian-country style. Deluxe accommodations and amenities with Puget Sound views.
• 705 N 5th • villabb.com ⓴

Satellite Coffee

A groovy little coffee shop that serves dialed-in espresso drinks made with beans from Portland's award winning Stumptown Coffee. Also serves delicious pastries and offers outdoor seating.
• 817 Division Ave. • 253.753.5858
• coffeetacoma.com ⓴

Old Town

Old Town was to be the hub from which Tacoma would grow, but when the railroad terminated a couple of miles away, the growing city's commercial district moved on up the road, leaving Old Town a Slavic/Swedish fishing village. Today it is a charming 3 block stretch along North 30th Street that boasts casual dining and drinking establishments, coffee houses, professional services, art galleries, parks and more.

John Idstrom

Spar Tavern/Coffee Shop

Righteous, reasonably priced pub grub focusing on burgers, sandwiches, fish and chips, soups and salads. Multiple beers on tap and bottled. Live music on Friday and Saturday. The coffee shop side is family friendly. • 2121 N 30th St.
• 253.272.2122
• the-spar.com

Cafe Divino

Cozy, casual wine bar with around 20 revolving wines by the glass and over 100 bottles to choose for either on-site or purchase. Extensive menu ranging from nibbles to full meals.
• 2112 N 30th St.
• 253.779.4226
• www.cafedivinotacoma.com

Hawthorn Tea Room

For those who know – or want to learn - the difference among High Tea, Lunch Tea, and Cream Tea. White linens and bone china teacups predominate. White gloves optional. Last seating at 3:00.
- 2208 N 30th St. • 253.238.9021
- thehawthorntearoom.com

Old Town Park/Job Carr Cabin

This pleasant park is home to the recreated cabin of Tacoma settler Job Carr, as well as numerous music and art festivals throughout the year. The Carr Cabin Museum recounts the history of the neighborhood and its early days as a Slavic fishing village.

Gateway Park

Located at the eastern end of the Old Town strip on N 30th and Starr, this pocket park has a couple of picnic tables, benches and killer views of Brown's Point and Vashon Island.

Throwing Mud Gallery

A chance to throw a pot, take a class or purchase artfully crafted ceramics made by experts. • 2210-2212 N 30th St. • 253. 254.7961
- throwingmudgallery.com

Ambrosia Florist

When cellophane-wrapped flowers from the grocery just won't do, Ambrosia will build a custom bouquet that fits the bill. For pick-up or delivery,
- 2210-2212 N 30th St.
- 253.272.2636
- ambrosiaflorist.com

Old Town Bicycle

A serious bike shop for people who are serious about cycling. These guys know their spokes and will help find the perfect ride. Sales and service only, no rentals.
- 3009 McCarver St. (basement of the Spar Tavern). Also in Gig Harbor and Olympia.
- 253.573.9400
- oldtownbicycle.com

Bluebird Boutique

Casual women's fashions and accessories, new and lightly used.
- 2209 N 30th St.
- 253.221.2156

Proctor District

Proctor is the heart of Tacoma's North End and an archetype of neighborhood shopping districts. Proctor hosts unique retail, a range of restaurants and historic landmarks. Tree lined streets and the pedestrian- and family- friendly atmosphere make this is a great place to explore. It's life lived mall-less and well.

Carolyn Burt

United Mason Methodist Church
Stained glass windows were created by Gabriel Loire of Chartres; he combines traditional and modern themes. Call for viewing hours.
- 2710 N Madison St.
- 253.759.3539
- masonchurch.org ❶

Blue Mouse Theater
Washington's oldest continuously operating movie theater, opened in 1923. On the National Register of Historic Places. Dale Chihuly designed the neon blue mice scampering across the facade. Second-run films, international film festival, community events.
- 2611 N Proctor St. • 253.752.9500
- bluemousetheater.com ❷

Proctor Art Gallery

Emphasis on Puget Sound artists working in oils, acrylics, watercolors, bronzes, fabric, wood, pottery, jewelry and more. Artists staff the gallery. • 253.759.4238 • 3811 N 26th • proctorartgallery.com ❸

Mason Plaza

Statue of pioneer Allen C. Mason by Paul R Michaels, surrounded by six sandstone columns from his mansion. Commemorates Mason's vision and role in Tacoma's development. His outstretched hand is shaken for luck. • Corner of N Washington St. and N 26th

Green Cape Cod
Bed and Breakfast

Quaint Cape Cod style B&B in walking distance. Also convenient to the University of Puget Sound, downtown and waterfront. Excellent home cooked breakfast, warm hospitality. • 2711 N Warner • 866.752.1977 • greencapecod.com ❹

Metropolitan Market

An upscale grocery open 24 hours; unique products from local vendors and around the world. Known for wines, pastries and take-out. Service and merchandising are outstanding; the staff does workshops for other businesses; grocers on tour study the store. • 2420 N Proctor • 253.761.FOOD • metropolitan-market.com ❺

Puget Park

Park toys and picnic tables. The adventuresome can hike down through Puget Gulch to Ruston Way and the waterfront, though people sometimes live in the Gulch. • 3111 N Proctor • 253.305.1000 • metroparkstacoma.org ❻

Anna Lemon Wheelock Public Library

Some claim to have seen the ghost of Anna McCormick for whom the library was first named; she was apparently upset when the library was renamed for Ms. Wheelock. These reports are vague on details. • 3722 N 26th St. • 253.617.7811 • tpl.lib.wa.us ❼

Chalet Bowling Alley One of the area's oldest family owned bowling alleys, newly renovated. Twelve lanes, cafe, strange bowling events. • 3806 N 26th St. • 253. 752.5200, • chaletbowl.com ❽

Pacific Northwest Shop

The shop features regional products including specialty foods, household decor, books, Native American designs, wines, candy, Mt. St. Helens volcanic ash art glass and more. Gift boxes shipped worldwide. • 2702 N Proctor • 800.942.3523 or 253.752.2242 • pacificnorthwestshop.com ❾

Giardini Gifts

Unique home accessories, personal care items, women's apparel, jewelry, stationery, ceramics, table ware and linens, glass ware, children's clothing, and garden decorations.
• 3815 N 26th St. • 253.759.0077
• proctordistrict.com ⑩

Jasminka

Women's shoes and clothing with a World Music vibe. Sized for real women.   Scarves, purses, jewelry and other accessories.
• 3820 N 26th St. • 253.752.8700
• jasminkatacoma.com ⑪

Tacoma Trains and Hobbies

Full service model train store and plastic and die cast models, rockets, kites and hobby supplies.
• 3813 N 26th St. • 253.756.7517
• tacoma-trains.com ⑫

Chirp & Company

Pet and garden store; remarkable variety of wild bird seed, squirrel food, bird and hummingbird feeders, garden art, gifts; dog and cat supplies. • 3803 N 26th St.
• 253.759.2884 ⑬

Wag Pet Market

Unusual and possibly luxurious accessories for pets. Wardrobe and play needs, natural, holistic and grain-free food & treats. • 2703 N Proctor • 253.756.0294 ⑭

The Harp & Shamrock

Fine Irish imports including linens, clothing, ceramics, jewelry and gifts. The oldest shop in Proctor. • 2704 N Proctor • 253.752.5012 ⑮

Teaching Toys and Books

Quality toys that support the emotional, physical, and intellectual growth of children. Also durable and safe, which matters too. Trained staff understands age-appropriateness. Gift wrap.
• 2624 N Proctor S • 253.759.9853
• teachingtoysandbooks.com ⑯

Old House Mercantile

Specializes in Fiesta ® dinnerware and unusual accessory pieces, English bone china, Polish pottery, candles, table decor; also skin care, stationery, and jewelry. • 2717 N Proctor • 253.759.8850
• oldhousemercantile.com ⑰

Historical Sidewalk Plaques

Designed and created by artist Paul R. Michaels; plaques describe history of the neighborhood. Found along N 26th and N Proctor Streets.
• michaelsbronze.com

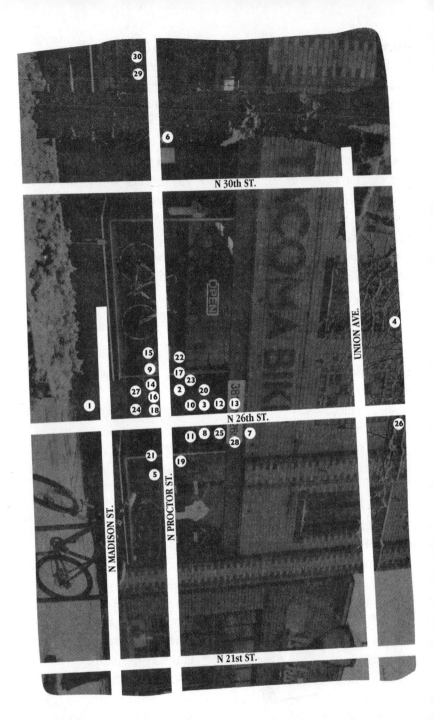

La Fondita

Family owned Mexican restaurant; varied and authentic cuisine and inviting atmosphere. Full bar.
- 2620 N Proctor
- 253.752-2878 **18**

Europa Bistro

Italian(Neapolitan) menu, baking daily; wine bar; outdoor seating in good weather.
- 2515 N Proctor • 253.761.5660
- europabistro.net **19**

Pomodoro

Small family run Italian restaurant; full bar. Reservations suggested. Open window and sidewalk seating in good weather. • 3819 N 26th St. • 253.307.8476 • pomodoroproctor.com ⓴

East and West

Thai and Vietnamese dishes; large menu for a small restaurant. Nice variety of noodle, rice, and hot dishes. • 2514 N Proctor St. • 253.756.5092 ㉑

Staircase Cafe

Casual lunch by day, upscale steak-and-seafood menu at night. Views and vintage decor. • 2717 N Proctor St. • 253.759.7336 ㉒

Knapps

Restaurant and lounge. A Proctor icon, serving since 1933. Family atmosphere with quality home style menu. Friendly staff, as in "more coffee, hon?" The Roberts' favorite spot Christmas morning. • 2707 N Proctor St. • 253.759.9009 • knappstacoma.com ㉓

Capers Cafe & Take Home

Premade meals with the quality of a chef-owned restaurant. Cozy dining for fresh soup and sandwich, or take out. Catering and boxed lunches available. • 2602 N Proctor, Suite D • 253.756.4444 • caperstakehome.com ㉔

Pour at Four—A Wine Bar

Nice selection of tapas, appetizers, salads and small plate entrees, artisan cheese selection, wide variety of local and European wines. Staff is well-educated, certainly on wine but also other things. Tastings. • 3814 N 26th St. • 253.761.8015 • pouratfour.com ㉕

Rosewood Cafe

From light meals to feasts for the hearty appetite. Extensive wine list. Rotating creations from local artists featured in the cafe. Great kids menu, excellent service and reasonable prices. • 3323 N 26th St. • 253.752.7999 • rosewoodcafe.com ㉖

Babblin' Babs Bistro

4 stars, with the chef as auteur. Euro / French- inspired menu. Intimate dining area. Special "Chef and I" dinners. Reservations suggested. Extensive gourmet breakfast and lunch selections. • 2724 N Proctor • 253.761.9099 • babblinbabs.com ㉗

Proctor Farmers' Market

Fresh local produce, cheeses, artisan breads, flowers, herbs, and garden decor. Live entertainment. Kids' booth. Located between North Madison and Proctor Street on North 27th • 253.961.3666
• proctorfarmersmarket.com

Tacoma Bike

Custom fitting bikes to customers. Free bike demos & seminars. Extensive inventory of clothing and biking supplies. Maintenance and repair. • 3816 N 26th St.
• 253.327.1118
• tacomabike.com **28**

GardenSphere

Urban dirt, with chickens scratching and a nice variety of seasonal plants. The young owners are serious about both the birds and horticulture; they're knowledgeable and take the time to understand what customers want. Even when the customer may not be sure.
• 3310 N Proctor • 253.761.7936
• gardensphere.biz **29**

Terry's Office Tavern

We get it: "stuck at the office, honey." Yeah yeah. Could be worse; folks have been working late here since 1936. Good traditional bar food, relaxed atmosphere.
• 3410 N Proctor • 253.752.6262
• terrysofficetavern.com **30**

University of Puget Sound

For strolling landscaped gardens or taking in a flute recital, the University of Puget Sound welcomes visitors to exhibits and performances, public art and some of the best-deal meals in town. 1500 North Warner, 253.879.3100; events calendar at pugetsound.edu.

Sharon Styer

Buildings and Grounds

Tudor-Gothic architecture hints at the medieval: elegant bay windows, square turrets, iron-hinged wood doors and rooftop garrets, all in brick buildings lined by lawns. The student garden along Alder at N. 16th is a relaxed contrast with the trim triangular plots elsewhere on campus. The giant sequoia in front of Wheelock Student Center is well-known, but it's only one of about 800 trees on campus including American beech, red filbert, and two kinds of cherry; a grove was planted by Japanese-American students re- located during WWII.

Music

The University's main music performance venue is Schneebeck Concert Hall (built 2002); it's home to the Jacobsen Performance Series with faculty, alumni, and guest artists as well as student productions, festivals, and workshops. Tickets at ups.universitytickets.com.

Kilworth Chapel

The Chapel's stained glass windows span two stories; the organ - made in Tacoma by Paul Fritts – commands the front wall. The Chapel hosts the monthly Organ at Noon series and is a performance favorite because the stage is set low and seating is intimate.

Collins Memorial Library

Built in 1954, Collins houses over 400,000 books and 130,000 periodicals. Collins hosts events and displays by the Puget Sound Book Artists, including regular exhibits of hand-made pieces.

Kittredge Gallery

The gallery is co-curated by Tacoma Art Museum and the University and displays prominent Northwest and national artists as well as student and staff work.

Public Art

Most notable is a three-story glass installation by Dale Chihuly (UPS '63). Created in 1990, it's in the north windows of Wyatt Hall and honors retired president Dr. Phillip Phibbs. Collins Library is the permanent home for the Abby Hill Collection with paintings, works on papers, and ephemera of this early Tacoma artist; professor-emeritus Ronald Fields led the revival of interest in Hill's work.

The most moving public art on campus may be Foucault's pendulum in Harned Hall's main lobby. The pendulum hangs over an inlaid wood base, tiled in shapes invented in the 1970s by physicist Roger Patterson.

Also in Harned Hall: a gray whale skeleton suspended from the ceiling. The skeleton is from a 14 month old, 27 foot long male Gray Whale found dead near the mouth of the Columbia River in 1973.

The Analemma clock and calendar uses the sun's rays to determine date and time.

Wheelock Student Center

Wheelock serves a wide range of food; visitors are welcome.

• The Chef's Table offers entrees and sides including seasonal vegetables.
• The Vegetarian/Vegan station is one reason UPS is consistently listed as one of the country's "Most Vegan-Friendly Colleges."
• Pacific Rim features pan-Asian food.
• Coffees and teas at Diversions Cafe
• and the Cellar, a student-run pizza house.

Bookstore

Not just text books. UPS gear, art supplies, popular fiction and nonfiction. Curiously, the bookstore is a trove of lovely - affordable - scarves. Hours vary.

The Sound, KUPS, 90.1 Eclectic programming 24/7 and a good source for what's happening on campus. KUPS was named Best College Radio Station by MTV in 2010.

Athletics

Logger athletic teams consistently advance to postseason competition. With 11 men's and 12 women's teams, watch D-III football, basketball, baseball and softball, tennis and lacrosse. For personal workouts, a quarter mile track is in Baker Stadium at Union and N 11th; the campus perimeter is 1.35 miles.

Vicci Martinez' Favorite Live Music Spots in Tacoma

I of course love **Jazzbones**. Reed Riley was the former booker and always brought great music to Tacoma. He left for a few years but he's back now and bringing more great live music.

Other places I like a lot include:

The New Frontier Lounge (301 E 25th St.)
Metronome Coffee (corner of 6th & Union)
The Tempest (913 MLK; thetempestlounge.com)
The Swiss (1904 Jefferson; theswisspub.com)

Vicci Martinez is a singer/songwriter from Tacoma. She records for Universal Group and came in joint third on NBC's The Voice in 2011.

6th Avenue

Tacoma's Restaurant Row upon Row upon Row. From holes- in- the- wall to beat-down taverns to elegant five star dining, 6th Avenue - especially the space between the five-way intersection of Sprague, Division and Sixth all the way to Proctor - where fork meets mouth in so many delectable, redoubtable, shout it from the rooftop ways. There's a Tuesday Farmers Market at the corner of 6th and Pine. Wild and wooly weekend music nights where youth and love reign supreme. There's the Mac Daddy of the Avenue, Chef Charlie McManus (they don't come any cooler than Chef), the first to put down roots in the upscale yet not out of reach category with his and wife Jacqueline's signature Primo Grill. There's Hot Yoga right on the other side of Proctor. And Sushi Tama next to it, greeting guests like long lost friends. To get from the intersection to Proctor can take some time. It's worth it. In between are treats and twists and surprises galore.

Rosalind Bell and Janet Thiessen

It's Greek to Me

Like a good neighbor: reliable, kind, always there with the falafel, the gyro, the spanakopita, hummus, calamarakia, the fries. Yes, the Greek fries! The portions are generous; the space not so much. Drive- thru or park.
• 1703 6th Ave. • 253.272.1375 ❶

Southern Kitchen

Satisfaction is the mark of patrons on their way out of here. Belly rubbing, belt loosening sighs of delight. The Soul Food gospel: fried chicken, fried catfish, collard greens, mac 'n cheese, corncake, red beans and rice...well, that's enough to get started. Oh wait, breakfast too.
• 1716 6th Ave. • 253.627.4282
• southernkitchen-tacoma.com ❷

MSM Deli

A classic case of not judging a book by its cover: the building housing this sandwich shop acts more as a deterrent to entry for those not in the know. Be in the know. Get in here! 50 eleven thousand hundred dozen types of sandwiches made to order. Beers from you name it. Wine too. People watching right up there with the best of them. • 2220 6th Ave. • 253.272.4814
• msmdeli.com ❸

DOA

If you have the cojones to name your restaurant DOA the food better be good. Well, the verdict is in: Guilty. The vittles are inspired!

Take for instance the breakfast: Habanero Shrimp and Sausage Benedict or Braised Elk Hash. Not into meat? There's this: Vegan Hash (squash, asparagus, mushroom, shallot, tomatoes, red bell pepper) with home fries. Their chicken and waffles would make Mildred Pierce and Roscoe swoon. Adult beverages abound and are also swoon-inducing. • 2309 6th Ave.
• 253.572.0588
• dirtyoscarsannex.com ❹

Feeling Smitten

"Hey Cupcake! Over here...get in... the tub...with me!" Thanks to Ms. Oprah, the world is beating a path to this 6th Avenue crown jewel: lusciously fragrant (natural ingredients, essential oils) Bath Bombs in the shape of cupcakes. And ice cream cones...And lollipops! Guilt-free; they're no-cal. • 2503 6th Ave.
• feelingsmitten.com ❺

Gateway To India

Travel the world and there's no warmer presence than CJ, co-owner of this Northern Indian, family-friendly restaurant. Samosas, papadams, curries, baingan ka bharta, vegetarian dishes, seafood, chicken, lamb, tandoori, biryani; a small sampling of what's in store. Daily buffet. • 2603 6th Ave.
• 253.552.5022
• gatewaytoindiarestaurant.com ❻

Studio 6 Ballroom

Get your dance on! Ballroom, Latin, swing, jazz, zumba workout! There's a main ballroom where happy feet become delirious. A private learning room for 'not quite ready for prime time' feet, a lounge area for feet too pooped to keep popping! Fun is the name of this game. No partner? No problem.
• 2608 6th Ave. • 253.905.5301
• studio6ballroom.com ❼

Cafe Dei

The irretrievably hip, the earth savers, the seekers, the yearners, the banker, the baker, the candle-stick maker all find their way to this robust coffee shop. Many come for the Spicy Chai Soy Latte! It's vegan and gluten free. Cooking classes for raw food lovers...or the curious. Call ahead to make sure they're open... hours are off. Sometimes.
• 2607 6th Ave. • 253.572.2550 ❽

Chopstix

Two pianos going at it for all they're worth. Jerry Lee Lewis. Ray Charles. Elton John. Booze. Food. BIG. LOUD. FUN. • 2702 6th Ave.
• 253.627.7555
• chopstixpianobar.com ❾

JazzBones

Sushi* Open Mic*Live Music* Pizza* Happy Hours* Ladies Night* Short Ribs* Tacos* Salads* Full Bar* Dancing Encouraged*
• 2803 6th Ave. • 253.396.9169
• jazzbonestacoma.com ❿

Medi's Pizza and Pasta

They might as well add Calzones... That's what's here, plus a variety of salads, karaoke, micro brews and Craterlake Root Beer. Pizza by the slice. Kid friendly... during the day... after hours is a whole 'nother ball of dough.
• 2710 6th Ave. • 253.272.2531 ⓫

Crown Bar

Don't often hear the words, "organic, locally sourced bar" in the same sentence. Maybe never. Except thru the door of The Crown Bar. This is the feisty little sister to Primo Grill, the Grande Dame of 6th Avenue's restaurant row. And like the best li'l sisters, this one has a mind of her own: All Day Sunday Happy Hour* Crispy Onion Burgers* Currywurst* Kebobs* Cajun Shrimp* Chocolate Pot Au Creme. Chef Charlie takes this 'every day' food every bit as seriously as the makings at Primo Grill. Goodness gracious, food this good should be against the law! • 2705 6th Ave.
• 253.272.4177
• crownbartacoma.com ⓬

Marrow

Enchanting. Ingenious. Zen-like. Unassuming. Marrow has altered the landscape of dining in tacoma. There is a wizard with a wand standing near the stove. Or a genie. There must be. Prediction: lines around the corner. Vegetarian and not. • 2717 6th Ave. • 253.267.5299
• marrowtacoma.com ⓭

Primo Grill

This is the old lady...venerable as she wants to be...the progenitor, the one who started all the fuss, the noise, the commotion about Destination 6th Avenue Dining! From globe-spanning cooking classes (Italy, Mexico, North Africa, Southern France) to pork chops that know no equal, to wood-fired pizzas this place dazzles. A truism: Unless the extraordinary evolves it will become ordinary. This old lady reinvents herself. Visionary Chef Charlie; extraordinary to the core.
• 601 S Pine • 253.383-7000
• primogrilltacoma.com ⓮

Red Hot

The FOOD NETWORK has discovered this place (Yes, ready for their close- up, Mr. DeMille) yet they have feet planted still in terra firma. But their dogs (even the veggie ones) are other worldly. And the beers! The beers!
• 2914 6th Ave. • 253.779.0229
• redhottacoma.com ⓯

Tacoma Food Coop

They have everything Whole Foods has except the hassle of driving to Seattle and leaving your paycheck at the register. Oh, and black rice (the new brown rice) in bulk.
• 3002 6th Ave. • 253.627.3344
• tacomafoodcoop.com ⓰

Laughing Lotus

The vibe here is um...very Om-mmm. Good. Good feelings. Hard not to smile when picking up a rain stick. Stuff (furniture, garden decor, rugs, jewelry, toys) from Afghanistan, Indonesia, Mexico, Vietnam, the Pacific Northwest. Baskets and hammered copper from Pakistan, masks carved in Java, beadwork handcrafted in Bali, rain chains from India, ceramics from Peru. Fairly traded, sustainable, and green handcrafted products purchased from artisans in villages around the world. • 3013 6th Ave.
• 253.627.0522
• laughinglotustacoma.com **⓱**

Engine House #9

Better than average tavern menu in a historic fire station. Burgers are tastier since the Asado/Masa folks took over. Craft beers brewed on site; full bar in back; event room upstairs. Several big screens show multiple sporting events. Kids welcome. • 611 N Pine
• 253.272.3435 • ehouse9.com **⓲**

Asado

Successfully modeled on an Argentine steak house, this is a popular spot for mesquite grilled meats and seafood; the beef is all natural Black Angus. Asado probably has the northwest's best selection of Argentine wines. Warning: the bar fills fast for happy hour. Super service. • 2810 6th Ave. • 253.272.7770
• asadotacoma.com **⓳**

Masa

Across the street from its sister Asado, Masa features a mix of traditional and innovative Mexican fare. Tacoma's biggest selection of tequila; deeper in the night Masa becomes a vibrant dance club, possibly related to the tequila.
• 2811 6th Ave. • 253.254.0560
• masatacoma.com **⓴**

Old Milwaukee

A smallish family-friendly spot with the accent on breakfast. One of those really strong mid-West accents, with huge portions and signature pies. It's not fast food but worth slowing down for.
• 3102 6th Ave. • 253.761.2602 **㉑**

Silk Thai

A large gracious room, unusual beer and wine variety and a well-executed menu. • 3401 6th Ave. # F **㉒**
• 253.756.1737 • silkthaicafe.com

BlueBeard Coffee Roasters

Spiritual home to the South Sound Users Guide and a lot of hipsters, especially those who hate the name. Great place to plug in and work or whatever.
• 2201 6th Ave. • 253.272.5600
• bluebeardcoffee.com **㉓**

Cork

An intimate little wine bar with a rolling selection, tastings, patio seating – and now Dulce Cupcakes.
• 606 N State St. • 253.212.5593
• corkwinebars.com **㉔**

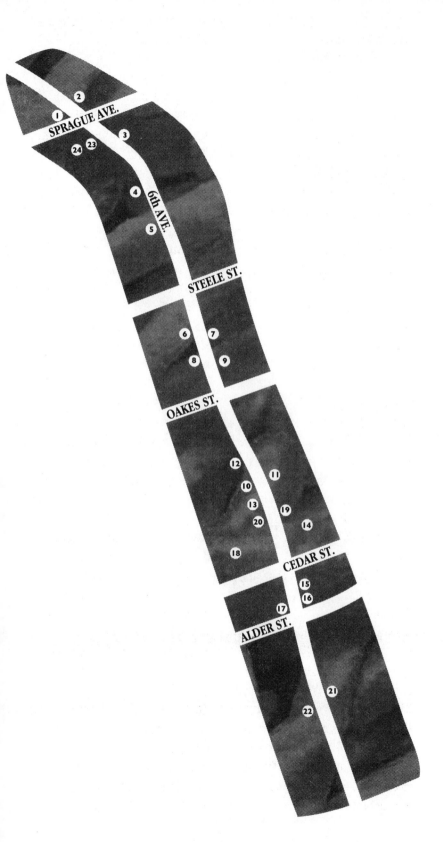

RUSTON WAY

Tacoma's year-round promenade, Ruston Way provides over two miles of wide sidewalk and panoramic views. In decent weather dog walkers, stroller pushers, runners, 'boarders and bicyclists share the path. Restaurants, small beaches, piers, public art and pocket parks dot the waterfront. And speaking of the view, on any given day... the Olympic Mountains, seals, bald eagles, scuba divers, Tall Ships, the Vashon ferry, freighters from around the globe, para-sailors, Mount Rainier, great blue herons, a fireboat pumping water, a dozen dog breeds, orcas and - rarely - Mount Baker.

Rebecca Young

Chinese Reconciliation Park

The park commemorates the 1885 expulsion of Tacoma's Chinese citizens and expresses hope for a more harmonious future. Fuzhou Pavilion (Ting) was donated by one of Tacoma's sister cities.
• 1741 N Schuster Parkway ❶

Sundial Park

This large steel sculpture tells the time; at the junction of Schuster Parkway and Ruston Way.
• 1895 N Schuster Parkway ❷

Northern Fish and Fish Tales Bistro

Clam chowder, Crab Louie or smoked and fresh fish all to go; a few benches. Dog water. (Also on South S 56th St.)
• 2201 Ruston Way • 253.272.4104
• northernfish.com ❸

Silver Cloud Inn

Part of a Seattle-based chain, this is Tacoma's only waterfront hotel, built out onto Commencement Bay; water views from all rooms. • 2317 Ruston Way • 253.272.1300 or 866.820.8448 • silvercloud.com ❹

Dickman Mill Park

The nine-acre park was a lumber mill from the 1890s until 1974. Beach access, walkways, wildlife habitat, public restrooms and mill remnants. • 2423 Ruston Way ❺

Harbor Lights

A Ruston Way fixture since 1959, Harbor Lights (purchased by Anthony's in 2000) is known for strong drinks and its four-pound bucket of clams. Which is a lot of clams. Early-bird menu. • 2761 Ruston Way • 253.752.8600 • anthonys.com ❻

Puget Park Trail

Puget Creek Restoration Society has been restoring 66 acres to a natural state; the trail goes between the Proctor District and Ruston Way. Volunteer opportunities.
• www.pugetcreek.org ❼

Katie Downs Waterfront Tavern & Eatery

Specializing in pizza and seafood, Katie Downs' big menu also offers charbroiled burgers, salads and appetizers. Deck dining.
• 3211 Ruston Way • 253.276.0771
• katiedowns.com ❽

Tidal Pool

Children love this imaginary tide-pool created by sculptor Bernhard Betz from mosaic seashells and natural rocks. It's in Knox Park outside Tacoma Fire Station No. 5.
• 3305 Ruston Way ❾

Fully Involved

Another sculpture near the fire station, by Larry Perkins, depicts three life-sized firefighters working to extinguish a blaze. It's part of a memorial to fallen firefighters.
• 3325 Ruston Way ❿

Duke's Chowder House

Duke's is part of a Puget Sound restaurant group specializing in chowder, salmon and other seafood dishes. • 3327 Ruston Way
• 253.752.5444
• dukeschowderhouse.com ⓫

Fireboat No. 1

After 54 years of protecting the waterfront, Fireboat No. 1 was drydocked and is now one of only five fireboats designated as National Historic Landmarks. ⓬

Les Davis Pier

A great place to fish or enjoy the fantastic view. The site is ADA accessible, with a concession stand.
•3325 Ruston Way ⓭

PAVE Bell

This bronze bell is decorated with cutout children. Created by Larry Anderson, the 4-foot-tall sculpture is accessible to all.
•3721 Ruston Way ⓮

Marine Park

The grassy expanse draws picnickers, sunbathers and volleyball players. Scuba divers gather for easy entry into the water. There's a U-shaped pier, flowerbeds and art.
•3931 Ruston Way ⓯

Cummings Park

Metro Park staff created this rock and flower garden at the end of Marine Park from huge rocks unearthed when Burlington Northern was installing a fiber optics line across the road. ⓰

Lobster Shop

Opened in Dash Point in 1977 and on Ruston Way in 1981, the Lobster Shop focuses on fresh seafood and offers Sunday brunch. Twilight specials. •4015 Ruston Way
•253.759.2165
•lobstershop.com ⓱

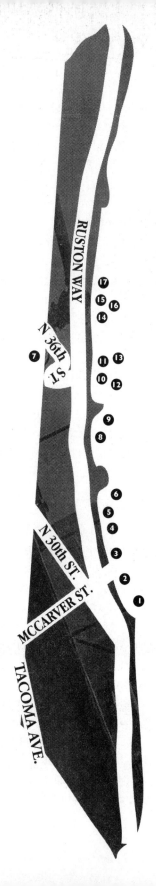

Town of Ruston & Point Defiance Park

Ruston incorporated in 1906, a distinct community sprung up around the smelting industry in the area. Named for the industrialist W.R. Rust, Ruston is less than half a square mile in size. Primarily residential, it also has a handful of unique businesses. For local going-ons presented by Ruston historian Karen Pickett: rustonhome.blogspot.com or rustonwa.org

Literally across the street and jutting into Puget Sound at Tacoma's northern tip, **Point Defiance** provides opportunities to engage with nature, regional history and culture. Noted in 1841 for its defensible geography, Point Defiance was designated a military reservation but never used by the military; it became a public park in 1888. The 702 acres encompass old-growth trees, historic buildings, gardens, trails, beaches, a zoo, and much more. The American Planning Association recently named the park one of the nation's "Ten Great Public Spaces." Open dawn 'til dusk.
• 5400 N Pearl St.

Kate Albert Ward

Don's Ruston Market and Deli

A locally run market since 1917, Don's features a 1940's era soda fountain where patrons slurp old fashioned sodas, milkshakes, malts and sarsaparilla. Good sandwiches too. •5102 N Winnifred •253.759.8151 ❶

W.R. Rust Playfield and Park

Atop a hill overlooking Commencement Bay, this park has a baseball backstop, large field, Big Toy, restrooms and a small sheltered area. Located on N Commercial St. just across the Winnifred Street Bridge from Don's Market. ❷

Winnifred Street Bridge

This span gives a clear view of Browns Point, Commencement Bay, and the Cascade Mountains. Below are the train tracks historically vital to Ruston.

Goldfish Tavern

A goldfish aquarium over the bar greets visitors who sidle up to order a beer. Billiards, comfortable bar stools, and a decent tap list make for happy regulars. •5310 N Pearl •253.759.7474 ❸

Antique Sandwich Co.

On the Ruston-Tacoma border, this eclectic Tacoma landmark offers fresh healthy food, fair- trade merchandise and a 22-year-old tradition of acoustic open mic night (Tuesdays; on tacoma.fm). •5102 N Pearl •253.752.4069 ❹

Jungle Fever Exotics

Hard-to-find plants for Pacific Northwest gardeners. A visit to this exotic oasis is a worthy adventure for novices and experts alike. •5050 N Pearl •253.759.1669 •junglefeverexotics.com ❺

Ruston Galleries

Antique items, such as jewelry, furniture, photos and books-- treasures for anyone with an affinity for objects from the past. •5114 N Pearl •253.752.8778 ❻

Divine Elegance Wedding Chapel

First dedicated in 1902, the building has had many names and uses through the years, including the Smelter Church. After four decades as an antique shop, it became a wedding chapel in 2006. •5129 N Pearl •253.228.0358 •divineeleganceweddingchapel. blogspot.com ❼

Tatanka Take-Out

A healthy fast-food option with a menu of lean, high-protein bison burgers and vegetarian fare. Perfect to pick up enroute to Point Defiance Park. •4915 N. Pearl •253.752.8778 ❽

Ruston Inn

This diner and lounge has dished out classic casual fare for forty years. Breakfast served all day; economical, simple and satisfying. •5105 N Pearl •253.752.3288 ❾

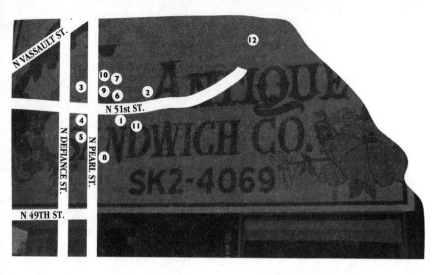

Point Defiance Cafe and Casino

For the lucky, and risk takers with a straight face. •5400 N Pearl •253.756.5101 ❿

Unicorn Sports Bar and Grill

Starting as a soft drink parlor during Prohibition, this building has long been a local imbibery, where folks meet to shoot the breeze and some pool. •5302 N 49th •253.752.5939 ⓫

Point Ruston (coming soon)

A planned community - complete with residences, shops, and recreation - located on the waterfront, where Ruston's former industries once operated. Small-town America of yesteryear meets contemporary urban development.
•pointruston.com ⓬

Ferry Terminal

The State ferry system is the largest in the U.S. This route runs to Vashon Island, with wooded roads, art galleries and a relaxed lifestyle.

The round-trip crossing is a pleasant hour in itself; drive on the ferry to explore Vashon; cycling is doable but vigorous.
•wsdot.com/ferries ⓭

Park Trails

This well-maintained trail network invites walkers and runners to explore the forest and enjoy coastal vistas. No trail head; refer to on line map for access. ⓮

Five Mile Drive

This forested road boasts sweeping views of the Narrows Bridge, mountain ranges, and other Puget Sound highlights; restricted to cyclists and pedestrians on weekends until 1pm.

Owen Beach

Driftwood is the seating on this rocky beach, with expansive views and tidal pools. Built amenities include a boardwalk, picnic shelters, public restrooms, free parking and kayak rentals. • 5605 Owen Beach • 253.305.1010 **⑮**

Fort Nisqually Living History Museum

The first European settlement in the Puget Sound, this 19th-century fur-trading post is enlivened by interpreters in period dress; admission fee; seasonal hours. 253.591.5339 **⑯**

Botanical Gardens

Local garden societies partner with park staff to cultivate dahlias, fuchsias, herbs, irises, and native plants. Varied blooming times mean color from spring through fall. **⑰**

The Rose Garden was founded with cuttings donated by school children in 1895. The Tacoma Rose Society now cares for over 1500 bushes that bloom June through September.

The Northwest Native Plant Garden displays over an acre of plants from various Northwest climates and geography. For guided tours, contact garden docents: nwnpgdocents@ tacomagardenclub.org

The Rhododendron Garden has more than 500 plants on five acres, celebrating the official Washington State flower.

The Dahlia Trial Garden. Here the Washington Dahlia Society tests new varieties from around the world before they're available to the public. Blooms all summer.

Pagoda and Japanese Garden

This 1914 building, stylized after a seventeenth-century Japanese Lodge, originally served as a streetcar station. A Japanese garden with water features surrounds the Pagoda. • 5801 Trolley Ln. • 253.305.1010

Lodge

Between 1898 and 1980, this Queen Anne style house served as a home for park officials. Today, event rentals keep the historic home busy year-round, as does its role as the Park's visitor center.
• 5715 Roberts Garden Rd.
• 253.305.1010 **⑱**

Marina

Boating and fishing classes, free public fishing pier, bait and tackle shop, motor boat rentals-- water enthusiasts of the world, come and enjoy! • 5912 N Waterfront Dr. • 253.591.5325 **⑲**

Anthony's at Point Defiance

A regional chain specializing in Northwest cuisine, fresh local seafood and waterfront views. A favorite post-beach stop for fish n' chips or clam chowder. • 5910 N Waterfront Dr. • 253.752.9700
• anthonys.com **⑳**

Public Art

The Park's art installations express Northwest heritage, history and values. The oldest (1925) honors founding-father Francis Cushman; in the newest (2005), local poets praise parks on the promenade.

Go Carts and Batting Cages For mechanical fun. •253.752.6413 •kartsandcages.com **㉑**

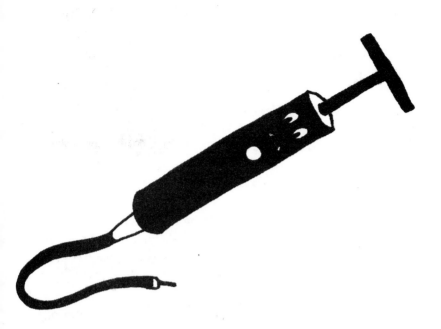

Great Bike Rides *by Dmitri Keating*

The rides I'd recommend depend on the riders and what they're looking for. But after surveying some of my riding friends I came up with a set of routes good for almost anyone.

Five Mile Drive at Point Defiance Park is an obvious choice. Safe, tree-lined roads, views of Puget Sound, wildlife, the Zoo, easy to find, lots of parking. It's just a huge win as far as I'm concerned. It's only five miles though which is short for lots of bicyclists. To make it longer, start by Dock Street at Thea Foss Park, ride the waterfront to Ferdinand and go up and over to the park from there. I've made a map of that ride here.....
mapmyride.com/routes/view/66761026

Easiest and very scenic ride is the Orting Trail. It's uphill on the way out but never steep at all. Kids do it all the time. Great views of the river and farmland around Orting plus a coffee shop at the end of the trail!
mapmyride.com/routes/view/806602

Short but hilly bike path can be found at Chambers Bay in University Place. Kids may have to walk the hills but the views are amazing and the beach combing at the bottom can add to the fun of the day.
mapmyride.com/routes/view/18009006

Boston Harbor in Olympia is a beautiful ride. A few great parks along the route and not very challenging hill-wise. Would be a hard ride for little kids but an average rider should have no problem with this route.
mapmyride.com/routes/view/66766532

Bike path over Narrows Bridge to Gig Harbor. Obviously the appeal to this ride is the view from the bridge. The rest of the route is not that hard and there are very few spots where a rider has to interact with traffic. It's an out and back but still a great ride.
mapmyride.com/routes/view/66770142

Vashon Island (south end from Point Defiance). Looking for a hard route? This would be my recommendation. Lots of hills but really pretty roads without much traffic. Beautiful ferry rides at the start and finish as well.
mapmyride.com/routes/view/7446763

Auburn to Flaming Geyser and Black Diamond Loop is a very pretty ride. Has one or two hard hills but is worth the effort. Plus the Black Diamond Bakery at the far end is awesome!
mapmyride.com/routes/view/66774716

Dmitri Keating *is co-owner of Old Town Bicycle, with shops in Gig Harbor, Tacoma's Old Town and Olympia.*

West End

The sleepy, suburban West End of Tacoma has some secrets. Breathtaking views of Puget Sound and unlikely urban parks are just a few reasons to spend the day at the other end of Sixth Avenue.

Shawn Cole

Cheney Stadium

An extensive renovation of Cheney Stadium in 2010 turned this historic fifty-year old ballpark into a premier venue for Triple A baseball. The Rainiers are a Mariner farm team so it's common to see big-leaguers on rehab and scouts in the stands. Ticket prices are still reasonable; great sightlines everywhere.
• 2502 S Tyler St. • 253.752.7707
• tacomarainiers.com ❶

Ben B. Cheney Statue

The man behind Tacoma baseball has the best seat in the house, thanks to local artist Paul Michaels. A life-sized bronze of Mr. Cheney, with peanuts and an opening-day scorecard, sits in the stadium that bears his name as a tribute to his dedication to baseball in his home town. ❷

75

The Tacoma Nature Center [Snake Lake]

Native plants and wildlife abound in this 70-acre wetland habitat with nearly two miles of trails and a nature themed play area. Guidebooks in the visitor's center explain the natural and historic significance of the land. • 1919 S Tyler St.
• 253.591.6439
• TacomaNatureCenter.org ❸

Tacoma Musical Playhouse

Producing quality musical theatre in Tacoma since 1994, the Playhouse is set in the Narrows Theater, built in 1948. The organization also sponsors trips and tours, and offers education for kids and seniors.
• 7116 6th Ave. • 253.565.6867
• tmp.org ❹

Tower Lanes

Love of the game inspired a group of Tacomans to renovate this 1950s landmark and turn it into a family-friendly fun center with bowling, miniature golf, billiard tables and an arcade. Restaurant and lounge.
• 6323 6th Ave. • 253.564.8853
• towerlanes.net ❺

The Cloverleaf

50 years of top-notch pizza, cold beer and free popcorn have made the 'Leaf a favorite for generations. Still in its original location; space for family dining and plenty of big screens for sports fans.
• 6430 6th Ave. • 253.565.1111
• cloverleafpizza.com ❻

WWII Memorial

Tacoma's salute to local troops features native gardens, monuments, a view of the Narrows Bridge and artifacts from Tacoma's military history including a 1902 ship's bell from the *USS Tacoma*. • 6th Ave. and S MacArthur St. ❼

Scott Pierson Bike Trail

Starting at South 25th Street, this 5-mile trail takes walkers and bikers through several West End nature areas, past Cheney Stadium, across the Narrows Bridge and into Gig Harbor. ❽

Titlow Beach

Once a campsite for the Puyallup and Nisqually tribes, Titlow Beach is a popular diving spot. Beach access for sunbathing and launching kayaks. Nearby Titlow Park has a picnic area, tennis courts, a playground and public pool.
• 8425 6th Ave. ❾

Titlow Lodge

In 1911 the Swiss style Titlow Lodge opened as a three story hotel. The work of architect Frederick H. Heath, who also designed Stadium and Lincoln High Schools, it's now a single story lodge available for rent; dance floor and kitchen.
• 8425 6th Ave. • 253.305.1010 ❿

Narrows Bridge
Walking or driving these twin suspension bridges on a windy day can make even seasoned South Sounders queasy, but the views are worth it. The two bridges make up the fifth longest suspension bridge in the U.S.; the Sound below is home to some of the largest octopi in the world. Drop-ins discouraged.
• 6th Ave. • 253.565.4692 ❿

Tacoma Boys
This locally owned market started as a seasonal stand on the side of the road after World War II, run by returning veterans. Now open year round, the market offers landscaping plants and Christmas trees [in season] as well as fresh fruits, vegetables and meats. Beer and wine.
• 5602 6th Ave. • 253.756.0902
• tacomaboys.com ⓬

Day Island
A cozy island village. The hidden but public trail leads to inspiring views of the Olympic Mountains and Puget Sound. ⓭

77

China Lake

Nestled next to a busy highway, this nature preserve hides one of Tacoma's largest lakes. Mostly un-developed, the trails and towering trees are a welcome surprise.
•S 19th and S Shirley ⓮

West End Tavern

Happy Hour specials, Karaoke and live Pay-Per-View events contribute to the local flavor of this neighbor-hood sports bar. The menu goes above standard tavern fare with a selection of steaks, ribs and whis-key-grilled chicken entrees. Full bar. •3840 6th Ave. •253.759.2896
•westendpubandgrill.com ⓯

Valhalla Coffee These folks have been roasting in Tacoma for almost ten years; they were kicked out of one location because the strong coffee fragrance disturbed a neigh-bor's clean air rights. Do the state nannies just drink tea or what? But okay, Valhalla's moved on and may be the area's best roaster. Grow-ing market penetration and a small retail operation.
•3918 6th Ave. •253.761.5116
•valhallacoffee.com ⓰

Joeseppi's Italian Ristorante

The Stortini clan has been serving home-style Italian dishes around Tacoma for generations. Joeseppi's maintains the tradition with a fam-ily-friendly atmosphere, fair prices and most important, excellent food. •2207 N Pearl •253.761.5555
•joeseppis.com ⓱

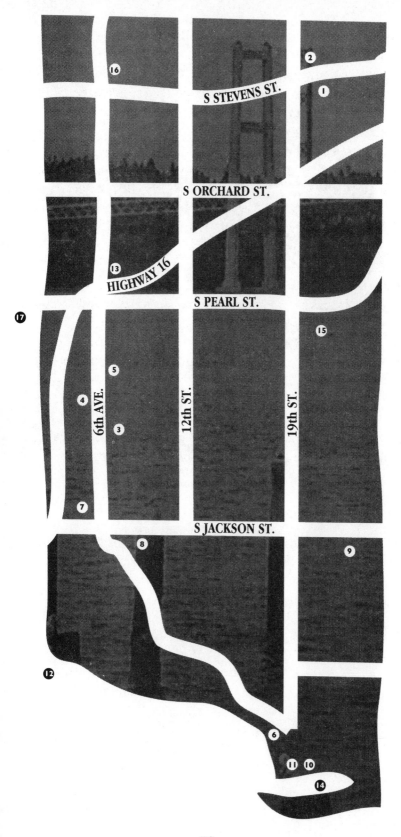

S STEVENS ST.

S ORCHARD ST.

HIGHWAY 16

S PEARL ST.

6th AVE.

12th ST.

19th ST.

S JACKSON ST.

Key Peninsula

Not far from the Purdy exit off Hwy 16, north of Gig Harbor, the historic Purdy Bridge crosses Burley Lagoon to a time when life moved at a slower pace. The Key Peninsula is 70 square miles of lush forest, parks, historic buildings and sweeping vistas of inlets and bays.

Barbara A Bourscheidt

The Purdy Bridge

Added to the National Register of Historic Places in 1982, this 550 foot hollow box girder bridge was the longest of its kind in the US when built in 1937. ❶

Minterbrook Oyster Company

The freshest, sweetest oysters in the Sound come from this bay-side operation. The web site is full of oyster-ish info.

• 12002 114th St. Ct. KPN
• minterbrookoyster.com ❷

Minter Creek Fish Hatchery
Operated by the Washington Fish and Wildlife Commission, this important salmon research hatchery features a small interpretive display. A great place to visit with kids.
• 12710 124th Ave. Ct. ❸

Glen Cove Hotel
Built in 1896, this homey Victorian resort overlooks quiet Glen Cove. It's open for bed and breakfast, tours and private functions. • 9418 Glen Cove Rd, KPN • 253.884.2835
• glencovehotel.com ❹

Ravensara Drive Through Espresso and Three Clouds Drive Through Bakery
The perfect stop – well, not a stop exactly; more a slowdown - for a cup to go, along with a cookie, muffin or loaf of artisan bread, baked on the premises! 11818 State Route
• 302 KPN • 253.853.3349 ❺

Blend
Specializing in NW Wines. $3.00 tastings on Fridays; selected glasses anytime. Knowledgeable, friendly proprietors, wine tasting dinners, poetry nights, and occasional music. • 8914 Key Peninsula Hwy
• 253.884.9688
• blendwineshop.com ❻

Key Peninsula Civic Center
Truly the hub of the community, this historic shingled building houses Friday Skate Nights, the Historical Society Museum, classes and art shows.
• 17010 S Vaughn Rd. KPN
• kpciviccenter.org ❼

Longbranch Marina
760 feet of public moorage; basic amenities and a covered gas barbecue area with storm curtains.
• Dock master: 253.884.1384
• longbranchimprovementclub.org/marina.php ❽

Home
Although no trace remains of the original anarchist colony [established here in 1895 and dissolved in 1919] the history is so interesting, it makes good reading over a picnic lunch! • en.wikipedia.org/wiki/Home_Washington ❾

Public Salt Water Boat Ramps
Boat ramps are available at Vaughn Bay, Home, Penrose State Park, Taylor Bay, and Joemma Beach State Park. • keypenpark.com

Public freshwater fishing
Jackson Lake and Bay Lake
• www.keypenpark.com

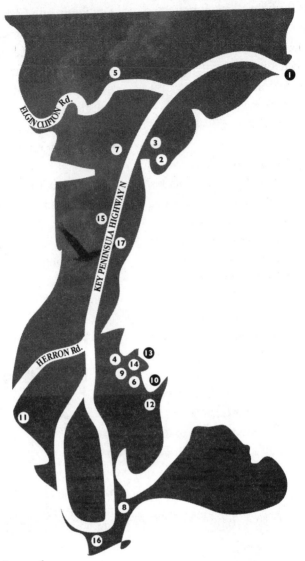

Penrose Point and Joemma State Parks

Among the best in the state park system, with saltwater access and opportunities to tent, hike, dig for clams and pick berries. Best to use maps on web sites for location information. • stateparks.com ⑩ ⑪

Volunteer Park

For Disc Golf, a stroll [careful of Disc Golfers] or a pit stop. This beautiful 20 acre park offers all three. Discs available for check out. • 5514 Key Peninsula Hwy N, Lakebay ⑫

Moosehead Cabin

On seven acres, with three bedrooms and capacity for up to 12 guests. Moose head in dining room [tasteful], secure high speed internet, dock with canoe and rowboat.
• 16202 Delano Rd. KPS
• mooseheadcabin.com ⑬

Trillium Creek Winery

Vintner Claude Gahard likes dry wines, perhaps because he's French; his wife, vintner Claudia Gahard likes fruitier bottles; her preference remains unexplained. They create both on site from grapes grown in Eastern Washington. Tasting room open year round.
• 17812 G St. KPN, Lakebay (about 12 miles from Gig Harbor proper).
• 253.884.5746
• trilliumcreekwinery.com ⓮

Blue Willow Lavender Farm.

Sells specimen plants, hosts weddings; educational field trips and tours. On summer Saturdays offers "Life on a Lavender Farm in Historic America" with costumed staff and talks. Open early April through late September. • 10615 Wright Bliss Rd., KPN • 253.225.9030
• bluewillowlavenderfarm.com ⓯

Creviston Valley Farm

A restored old-style cattle ranch focused on sustainability and community-supported agriculture. Farm products for sale. The farm participates in World Wide Opportunities on Organic Farms, offering internships to people interested in sustainable, organic farming. Tours available with a call in advance.
• 3421 Creviston Rd. KPS, Longbranch • 253.858.4844
• crevistonvalley.com ⓰

Close to Home Espresso

Hands down the best cup of joe on the KP. Batdorf and Bronson beans and friendly service. Pick up an 884 shirt! Located next to the grocery store in Key Center. ⓱

Gig Harbor

Picturesque Gig Harbor boasts a maritime past still evident today. Its quaint harbor, a photographers' delight, is home to fishing vessels and pleasure craft. The downtown center features historic homes dating to the latter 1800s. Once reached only by tiny private ferries, Gig Harbor is easily accessible from Tacoma by twin suspension bridges.

Meri Arnett-Kremian

The Inn at Gig Harbor
52 rooms, complimentary breakfast for guests. Fitness & business center. Wireless internet access. Non-smoking facility. Restaurant on property and several nearby.
• 3211 56th St. NW • 866.539.0036
• innatgigharbor.com ❶

Wesley Inn & Suites
Known for its friendly atmosphere. Spacious rooms with flat screen TVs, internet access, guest breakfast. Dog friendly, as long as they (and you) don't smoke. Pool.
• 6575 Kimball Dr. • 253.858.9690
• wesleyinn.com ❷

Maritime Inn

Scenic location in historic district. Across the street from a marina, so guests come by boat as well as car. Smoke-free, internet access, free parking. Continental breakfast. Special packages available.
• 3212 Harborview Dr.
• 253.858.1818
• maritimeinn.com ❸

Aloha Beachside Bed & Breakfast

5 guest rooms with private baths, feather beds, water views or balconies. Award-winning breakfasts with Hawaiian flair. Hosts small, intimate weddings. • 8318 State Route 302
• 1.888.ALOHABB
• alohabeachsidebb.com ❹

Heritage Restaurant (Inn at Gig Harbor)

Seasonal menu. Cozy atmosphere, moderate prices. ❺
• 3211 56th St. NW • 253.858.1111

Brix 25

Dinner only, 7 days a week; fine American cuisine with a Northwest flair; award-winning wine list. Reservations recommended.
• 7707 Pioneer Way • 253.858.6626
• harborbrix.com ❻

Devoted Kiss Cafe

Bright and airy; serves breakfast & lunch. Open 7 days from 6 am to 3 pm. • 8809 N Harborview Dr., Suite 203 • 253.851.0055
• devotedkisscafe.com ❼

Green House

Chef Robert Green showcases fresh, simple, seasonal food from local sources. An open kitchen lets you experience culinary fun. Dinner Tues – Sun. Wine list; children's selections. • 4793 Point Fosdick Dr. NW, Suite 400 (opposite Galaxy Theater at Gig Harbor Uptown center) • 253.514.6482
• greenhousegigharbor.com ❽

The Green Turtle

Owner Sue Glenn couples fresh seafood and meats with organic produce, served in a quaint dining room or on the outdoor deck, both with views of the light house-style beacon at the harbor entrance and majestic Mt. Rainier. Lunch and dinner. • 2905 Harborview Dr.
• 253.851.3167
• thegreenturtle.com ❾

Tides Tavern

Locals bike, drive and boat to the world-famous Tides, a kids-free hangout. Waterside deck tables are coveted in good weather. Occasional live music. Casual but tasty pub grub. Beer, wine, and spirits. In the heart of the historic downtown, this is the signature Gig Harbor place. • 2925 Harborview Dr.
• 253.858.3982 • tidestavern.com ❿

7 Seas Brewing

Innovative craft brewery making audacious beer while promoting environmental responsibility. Cans, not bottles, for lots of reasons they'll explain. Voted Best Brewery in South Sound (2011). 3207 57th Street Court NW in the shopping plaza at Judson Street and Soundview Drive. • 253.514.8129
• 7seasbrewing.com ⓫

Olalla Valley Vineyard

Tiny vineyard & winery on bluff overlooking Olalla Bay and Vashon Island. Family-run operation; "Croatian Family" label in honor of the vintner's heritage. No sulfites used after initial fermentation. Hours vary. • 13176 Olalla Valley Rd., Olalla (just north of Gig Harbor)
• 253.851.4949 ⓬

Destiny Harbor Tours

Daily one and two hour tours of local waters April through December. Winter tours by appointment; 4 person minimum. Private charters available. • 253.225.6306
• destinymarine.com

Gig Harbor Rent-a-Boat

Human-powered and motorized craft for rent including double or single kayaks, canoes, peddle boats. Guided kayak trips, private lessons, family kayak Sundays, and kids' kayak camps.
8829 N. Harbor View Dr.
253.858.7342 ⓭

Madrona Links Golf Course

The Harbor's only public 18-hole course. Club atmosphere; greens show loving care. Pro shop.
• 3604 22nd Ave. NW
• 253.851 5193
• madronalinks.com ⓮

Performance Golf Center

Sometimes life lacks ping without a swing. Here's a driving range and golf instruction plus miniature golf for more modest ambitions. Sited a par 5 from the Narrows Bridge.
• 2416 14th Ave. NW • 253.853.4653
• performancegolfcenter.com ⓯

Self-Guided Historical Waterfront Walking Tour

About a mile of mostly level sidewalk along the waterfront in the historic heart of town; good signage discusses Gig Harbor history.

McCormick Forest

122 acres of unspoiled forest with hiking, biking, and horse trails (horses not included). Over 3 miles of trails. McCormick Creek runs through the property.
• 10301 Bujacich Rd. NW
• penmetparks.org ⓰

Cushman Powerline Trail

Paved pedestrian trail on land paralleling Highway 16. A haven for walkers, joggers, roller bladers, and bicyclists. Trailhead with parking for cars located at 14th Ave. NW. There are benches, bike racks, and picnic tables along the trail. ⓱

Harbor History Museum

Permanent exhibition showcases Gig Harbor Peninsula history; several exhibitions each year. Small fee for non-members. Shortened winter hours. 4121 Harborview Dr.
• 253.858.6722
• harborhistorymuseum.org ⑱

Paradise Theatre

PLAY community theater features classic Broadway fare; Saturday dinner theater option. Senior/student/adult rates. • 9911 Burnham Dr.
• 253.851.7529
• paradisetheatre.org ⑲

Gig Harbor Galaxy Theater

Typical suburban multiplex except with an over-21 screening venue serving beer and wine. In the Uptown shopping plaza. • 4649 Pt. Fosdick Dr. NW • 253.857.7469
• galaxytheatres.com ⑳

Gig Harbor Farmer's Market

Food, flowers, arts and crafts Saturdays 8:30 – 2:00, April – Sept. in the northeast parking area of Gig Harbor Uptown shopping center
• 4649 Pt. Fosdick Dr. NW
• gigharborfarmersmarket.com ㉑

Summer Sounds at Skansie

Live music every Tuesday evening (rain or shine) at Skansie Brothers Park. Offerings range from swing to rock; marches to mariachi. We await a mariachi march. Lawn seating so a chair or blanket's advised; picnics okay but no smoking or alcohol..
• 3207 Harborview Dr.
• gigharborguide.com ㉒

Cinema Gig!

Classic films of the 1940's to 80's outdoors alternating Friday nights in summer at Donkey Creek Park (corner of Harborview Drive and N. Harborview Drive at 3-way stop). Family films the next night at Skansie Brothers Park. Gets cold [unless showing Farenheit 451]. Films show at dusk. Free, including popcorn. [Did we mention Some Like It Hot?] • gigharborguide.com

Java & Clay Cafe

In the front, beverages, tasty treats and conversation. In the back, mugs and platters to paint and pick up in a day or two. Suitable for kids and adults, with or without artistic tendencies. • 3210 Harborview Dr.
• 253.851.3277
• JavaClayCafe.com ㉓

Gallery Row

Cooperative gallery staffed by artists working in a variety of media. Heart of downtown. • 3102 Harborview Dr. • 253.851.6020
• gigharborgalleryrow.com

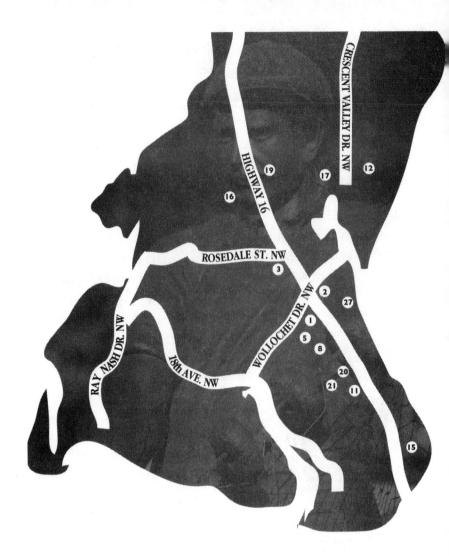

For Arts' Sake
Fine arts and crafts; jewelry; photography. • 3155 Harborview Dr.
• 253.858.8087
• forartsakeinc.com **24**

Beach Basket
Gig Harbor gift shop and women's clothing; year-round Christmas shop with all the trimmings next door. • 4102 Harborview Dr.
• 253.858.3008 **25**

Harbor Peddler
Home accessories and gifts; Northwest-made products. Oh, and huckleberry taffy! • 3311 Harborview Dr. • 253.851.6795 **26**

Misty Meadow Antiques
Vintage collectibles, including manly things. Closed Tuesday & Wednesday. • 6319 Soundview Dr. • 253.851.3800
• mistymeadowantiques.blogspot. com **27**

Mostly Books

Independent bookseller in historic district; strong in nautical and local history, maps. • 3126 Harborview Dr. • 253.851.3219
• mostlybooks.com ㉘

Gig Harbor Beads

Our string runneth over. A cornucopia of jewelry making supplies, with how-to classes. • 7700 Pioneer Way
• 253.858.6750
• gigharborbeads.com ㉚

Cottage at Gig Harbor

A modest 1930s fishing cabin. Of course it's modest. But remodeled and updated with WiFi and cable TV; great place to watch the Fishing Network. One bed and bath plus a sleeper sofa, kitchen and patio. And a great location, walkable to downtown. • 7614 Pioneer Way
• 406.249.1988
• gigharborcottage.com ㉛

Harbor Quilt

Classes, supplies and equipment for hard-core quilters. • 7716 Pioneer Way, Suite D • 253.743.9995
• harborquilt.com ㉙

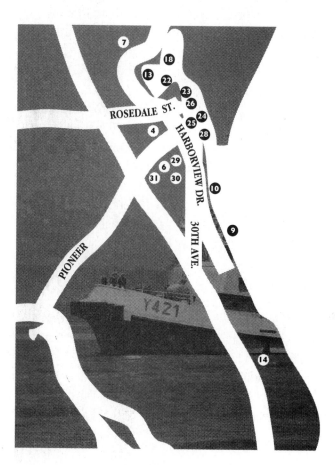

Fife

When Fife was incorporated in 1957 it was already the hub of a thriving agricultural zone. Now it's a gateway to the Port of Tacoma and home to manufacturing and warehousing, while keeping its neighborhood roots.

Jackie Fender

Poodle Dog

Traditional home cooking in a diner atmosphere? The Poodle Dog is the place to be. Serving up favorites like hotcakes and links, it's been an area staple since 1933. • 1522 54th Ave. • 253.922.6161 • poodledogfife.com ❶

Emerald Queen
Hotel & Casino

The Fife location is one of three owned and operated by the Puyallup Tribe. This site has three restaurants, gaming - duh - and entertainment. • 5700 Pacific Hwy. • 253.922.2000 • emeraldqueen.com ❷

Fife Swim Center

Large pool, smaller wading pool for the kiddies and a hot tub, all cleaned with salt water in lieu of the usual chemicals. • 5410 20th St. E • 253.922.7665 • cityoffife.org ❸

Dacca Park

A hidden gem, with baseball field, the Fife History Museum, playground, walking trails and even beach volleyball. With no beach. Weird. • 2820 54th Ave. E • 253.896.8652 ❹

Fife History Museum

Located in the home of a former city council member, the Museum holds public records, stories about the city's development and some historic characters [inert]. Outside sit a bright yellow caboose and engine, signaling Fife's ties to railroading. • 2820 54th Ave. E • 253.896.4710 ❺

Fountain Memorial

Both a park and historic landmark, the Memorial dates to 1914; recent plaque additions in 1988 in remembrance of Fife community figures. Nice spot for a sack lunch. • 2001 54th Ave. E

Pickwick Burgers

Classic burger goodness right here: bacon cheeseburgers, fountain drinks and ice cream shakes. Loads of picnic tables. The sometimes-long lines are testament to the popularity of a good burger. •4306 Pacific Hwy. E •253.922.5599 ❻

Wart Hog Barbeque Pit

Swathed in aromas, the Pit is a favorite destination for BBQ lovers. Ribs and brisket sandwiches among other offerings. •4921 20th St. E ❼ •253.896.5091 •warthogbbq.com

Bj's Bingo

Getcha daubers ready. Bingo, slots and pulltabs; 600 seats. Whew. Cafe and bar with table service. •4411 Pacific Hwy. E •253.922.0430 •bjs-bingo.com ❽

Johnny's at Fife

Reliably good food and service; strong sea food menu. Open early for breakfast; lounge with karaoke is not family friendly; the rest of the place is excellent for kids to eat in a "grown-up" place. •5211 20th St. E •253.922.6686 • johnnysatfife.com ❾

Paws-abilities

Sure, dog people go overboard sometimes but this place is reasonable. Really. Fitness center, camps, agility and sports training as well as prep to be comfort dogs in nursing homes. Okay, so this Rottweiler walks into a gym... •7338 26th St. E •800.730.3794 •everydoghas.com ❿

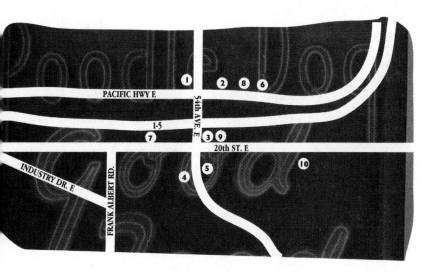

Parkland

Parkland is not, shall we say, a major destination in the South Sound. It's not flashy or grand, but it doesn't pretend to be, either. It's a working class community filled with folks who may or may not spend hours manicuring their yards, but who are real and true and living their lives. Parkland's main distinction is that for the past hundred-plus years it's been home to one of Washington's top private universities, **Pacific Lutheran**. Within the university bubble, sections of Parkland are decidedly beautiful and robust.

Jesse Michener

Scandinavian Cultural Center

Celebrating its Scandinavian roots, PLU houses the Scandinavian Cultural Center within the newly-remodeled University Center walls. Distinctive events happen throughout the year; the non-Scandinavian are usually welcome. • 122nd & S Park/University Center, Room #100 • 253.535.7532 • plu.edu/scancenter ❶

University Gallery

Mostly student-created art from PLU's prestigious Art Department. A rotating schedule assures something new almost every month. It's a little gem hardly anyone knows about. • Ingram Hall, Pacific Lutheran University • 253..535.7573 • plu.edu/art ❷

2121 Tavern

Known for good fried food and a long history. Pool, video games, and pull tabs.
• 2121 112th St. E • 253.536.2100 ❸

Marzano's Restaurant
The nicest place to eat near the university. Located in a converted house, the menu is sophisticated Italian. "Casual elegance" is apt.
• 516 Garfield • 253.537.4191 ❹

The Wagon Wheel Restaurant
A greasy spoon with an old-timey, country feel. Coffee is plentiful as are breakfast meats and crispy potatoes. They serve food all day, but breakfast is the big event.
• 11811 Pacific • 253.537.3211 ❺

Madea's Cajun Cafe
Simple, authentic - and crowded. Cause and effect may be at work. Chef and owner Keitha Okafor is a Louisiana native. Limited menu.
• 417 Garfield • 253.536.7060 ❻

The Northern Pacific Coffee Co.
A combination bookstore, coffee house, bar, concert venue, and community anchor in Parkland. Good eats, yummy treats and fine atmosphere. It's a winner.
• 401 Garfield • 253.537.8338 ❼

Franks Donuts
A regional favorite and well-loved donut house. People show up early, like really early, for the best selection. Stuff of the gods, Nordic division. • 14117 Pacific
• 253.535.4699 ❽

Pacific Avenue Antique Mall
An antique-lover's paradise. A visit to Pacific Avenue Antique Mall is like hunting for treasure (and probably finding some, too).
• 10228 Pacific • 253.539.0117 ❾

Hobbytown
The shop specializes in trains, rockets, RC and other geekly-wonderful model parts. • 402 Garfield
• 253.531.8111 ❿

Gonyea Playfield
Features multi-purpose fields, a playground and restrooms. It's a neighborhood gem, well-loved and used. • 13422 10th Ave. ⓫

Garfield Book Company
The PLU bookstore moved out into the community. An excellent idea. Along with textbooks and university gear, Garfield Books has a Scandinavian shop, good selection of general reading, special events and author appearances. • 208 Garfield
• 253.535.7665
• luteworld.plu.edu ⓬

Paradise Bowling Alley
Fun for the whole family and more. It's a bowling alley, a restaurant, a nightclub and an arcade. It's a little nuts. Sometimes that's good and sometimes it's just nuts.
• 12505 Pacific • 253.537.6012
• paradisebowl.net. ⓭

Parkland Putters

With four courses of varying difficulty levels, putts golfers to the test. It's a super-fun, kitschy place to spend a few hours. Also: they award prizes. Score!
• 10636 Sales Rd. • 253.588.2977 **⑭**

Yummers 2 the 3rd Power

Cupcakes can't be passe with flavors like these: maple French toast and bacon; sweet potato pie; PJ&B; Puerto Rican vacation. Yummers motto: cake, not the fluffy stuff. Indeed. • 317 Garfield
• yummers2the3rdpower.com **⑮**

Parkland Parish Quilts

A quilting community hub in a century-old church. Excellent fabric selection, helpful staff, lots of events and clubs.
• 12152 Pacific • 253.531.4309
• parklandparishquilts.com **⑯**

Jade Mountain Nursery

This is about bamboo – more than 50 varieties, from miniatures to towering timber. The staff is quite knowledgeable and has decades of experience using bamboo in landscaping. Jade Mountain also offers bonsai, Japanese maples, other ornamental trees and ornamental grasses. The nursery specializes in decorative trees for small spaces.
• 5020 116th St. E • 253.548.1129
• jademountainnursery.com

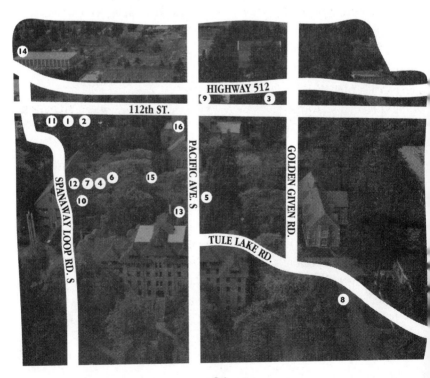

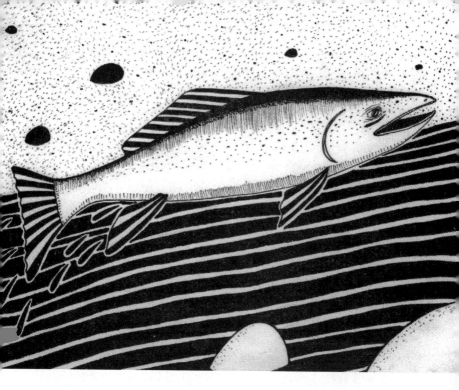

Puyallup

Puyallup is a town of almost 40,000; its fertile valley is in the shadow of Mount Rainier. The land and nearby river have provided fish, agricultural bounty and stunning vistas for centuries, long before Oregon Trail pioneer Ezra Meeker founded the town in 1877. Named for the Native tribe who called it home (Puyallup means "the generous people"), the community is still deeply connected to its agricultural past as it evolves from a sleepy, distant neighbor of Tacoma to a lively town with art, music and foodie scenes all its own.

Jesse Michener

Ezra Meeker's Mansion
Now a history museum. Pretty fancy after coming off the Oregon Trail and better than a covered wagon, for sure.
• 312 Spring • 253.848.1770
• meekermansion.org ❶

The Karshner Museum
Mostly used as a teaching museum and run by the Puyallup School District, the museum is open to the public for just two hours a day during the school year and on the first Saturday of each month. Worth a trip; it has an intriguing collection.
• 309 Fourth St. NE
• 253.841.8748
• karshnermuseum.org ❷

Mama Stortinis

A family-friendly Italian restaurant, offering good food, locally sourced when possible and reasonably priced. Gluten free and vegetarian options available. Related to Tacoma's Joeseppi's.
• 3207 E Main • 253.845.7569
• mamastortinis.com ❸

Comfort Food Cafe

Voted the 2010 Best of Western Washington's "Healthy Places to Eat Lunch", CFC offers farm-to-table breakfast and memorable lunch.
• 210 W Pioneer • 253.770.6147 ❹

Mike and Terry's Outdoor Sports Park

Two miniature golf courses, go-karts [age ten minimum for one type, age 16 minimum for the other], batting cages for hardball, softball and fast pitch. • 6326 114th Avenue Ct. E • 253.841.1234
• mikenterrys.com ❺

Casa Mia

This is one of several locations for this Washington restaurant group, started in 1952 by an Italian-American GI. The menu is pretty straightforward; the big draw is pizza, which keeps winning national awards. A sympatico spot for vegetarians. • 505 N Meridian
• 253.770.0400 • casamiarestaurants.com (also in Yelm, Lacey, Olympia and Lakewood.) ❻

Powerhouse Brewpub and Restaurant

One of the South Sound's early brewpubs, in a nicely re-used power generating station. The menu leans Italian and maritime; a root beer and seven non-root beers are brewed on site, including "Four Alarm Stout."
• 454 E Main • 253.845.1370
• Powerhousebrewpub.com ❼

Trackside Pizza

Handmade dough, premium cheeses, specialty meats and fresh herbs. Seems to work; there's a crowd of regulars.
• 201 N Meridian • 253.845.7437
• pizzatrackside.com ❽

HG Bistro

Steaks, seafood, pasta, delicious sliders and wagyu kobe burgers make HG Bistro the go-to spot for fine (but casual, not stuffy) dining in Puyallup. Sourced locally whenever possible. Also local art and musicians. • 1618 E Main
• 253.845.5747 • hgbistro.com ❾

The Puyallup Farmers Market

A downtown landmark. Running April – October on a variable Saturday/Sunday schedule, it offers a mix of artisan and agricultural fare, with a good vibe and community feel. Under a pavilion, which is useful on the rare misty day. • 330 S Meridian in Pioneer Park • 253.840.2631
• puyallupmainstreet.com

Puyallup's Historic Downtown

Recent revitalization efforts are paying off in the downtown corridor. Local merchants, food and outdoor events make this highly-walkable downtown special. The Main Street Association runs a nice little website and is a great resource for shopping, eating and events.
• 107 N Meridian • 253.840.2631
• puyallupmainstreet.com ❿

Watson's Greenhouse and Nursery

A pretty awesome place, even for non-green thumbs. Watson's has it all: stuff to grow, pretty trinkets, helpful people and a cafe. • 6211 Pioneer Way E • 253.845.7359
• watsonsgreenhouse.com ⓫

Antique Stores Puyallup

A respectable cadre of antique stores. Map available thru the Antique Dealers Association.
• www.antiquedistrict.net

Outdoor Art

Puyallup has one of the largest municipal collections of outdoor art in Washington, thanks to Arts Downtown. The collection includes 39 permanent installations.
• www.artsdowntown.org

Meeker to McMillan section of the Pierce County Foothills Trail

This four-mile span scats and jives amid trees and farms, alongside an active railway. The trailheads look like mini train stations. • 13810 80th St. in East Puyallup (edge of VanLierop Bulb Farm)
• co.pierce.wa.us ⓬

Puyallup Riverwalk Trail

Runs five miles from the city's western boundary to the East Main bridge, most of it along the river. Jog, bike, skate, whatever.
• cityofpuyallup.org ⓭

View With a Room

They're called Zoom and Lenny, and they run a View With a Room. Judging on the basic coolness of their naming conventions, this B&B wins. They promise great food, calm and stories, plus an unforgettable view. • 14608 136th Ave. E
• 360.893.8649
• aviewwitharoom.net ⓮

Clarks Creek

A wee tributary of the Puyallup River; adult salmon return to spawn each winter. Footbridges make viewing the salmon runs easier for everyone. The nearby fish hatchery is fun to tour as well. Open year-round, with peak chumming in December. • Between 15th Ave. SE and 14th St. SW
• wdfw.wa.gov/fishing ⓯

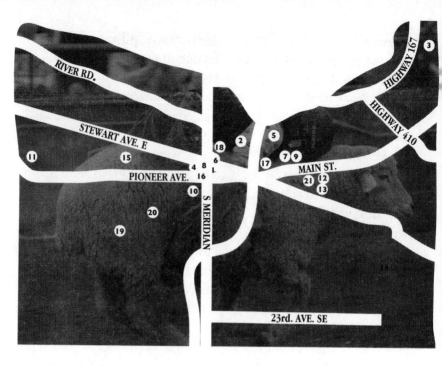

Pioneer Park

Puyallup's downtown park, with lots of bells and whistles and access to the library, City Hall and the Farmer's Market. It's got that center-of-the-universe feel - Puyallup's universe, at least. And many of the city parks are worth a look; they're well maintained and offer lots of recreation options: off-leash areas, skating, a sports complex and myriad playgrounds.
• cityofpuyallup.org ⑯

Liberty Theater

85 years old and nicely renovated. The Theater itself hosts events ranging from catered holiday celebrations to big-screen sports telecasts. Private sponsors host album launches and other music and drama. • 116 W Main
• 253.845.5105
• thelibertytheater.com ⑰

Tiffany's Skate Inn

Puyallup's roller-skate hub for 40 years. Public skating, equipment rentals and sales; available for parties. In-line racing team. Loud music. • 1113 N Meridian
• 253.848.1153
• tiffanysskateinn.com ⑱

Hedman House

A 1907 farmhouse with relaxing grounds; two bedrooms and adjoining bath, private bath option available. Private courtyard. • 502 9th St. SW • 253.848.2248
• hedmanhouse.com ⑲

Tayberry Cottage

Victorian home with elaborate breakfasts including soy milk and vegetarian options.
• 2718 9th Ave. SW
• 253.880.2200 ⑳

Quilt Barn

Fabrics classes, quilt shows and machine rentals. Tastes run to the traditional end of the spectrum.
• 2102 E Main • 253.845.1532
• quiltbarn.com ㉑

The Puyallup Fair

If the city was founded on agriculture, it got its reputation from the fairs it hosts. Puyallup's annual fall fair is the single biggest in the state, consistently drawing over a million visitors in its 17-day run in September. And, yes, the scones are that good. Rides, sure, but also the stuff which first brought folks out a hundred years ago: the craft and livestock shows, folk art and food. There's a smaller spring fair in April and the 169-acres fairgrounds are used year-round for events.
• 110 9th Ave. SW • 253.841.5045
• thefair.com

The Daffodil Festival

In the 1920's when crops failed, daffodils were planted and a thriving bulb and flower industry was born. In the 1930's, instead of being thrown out as fertilizer, the daffodil blooms were used to decorate cars and floats in what would become the Daffodil Parade. This much-loved yearly event winds through four cities - Puyallup, Tacoma, Orting and Sumner - and heralds the beginning of spring in the region. This does not necessarily mean sunshine; just spring. Annually, in April, with affiliated events year-round. daffodilfestival.net.

Sumner

Sumner is a delicious mix of tradition, family, celebration and the quaint-but-not-corny. Old fashioned diners with enormous slices of pie, lovingly preserved historic buildings, shops, clean safe parks, and community spirit make this town a gem. Downtown's Main Street offers free parking and walkability. The town comes alive with celebrations year-round, highlighted by Spring's Daffodil Parade. Sumner is a pleasure for antiquers, with blocks of specialty shops.

And Sumner is the rhubarb pie capitol of the world; many of the town's diners feature fresh baked pie. Oh yes. And ice cream.

Kim Thompson

New England Salt Box
With an antiques section inside, this store focuses on vintage and contemporary Americana, including furniture and decor, fabric and wallpaper. •1119 Main •253.826.3506 • newenglandsaltbox.com ❶

Whistle Stop Antique Mall
Who doesn't love antique shopping? Helpfully organized by type of goods.
•1109 Main
• 253.863.3309 ❷

Heritage Quest Research Library and Book Store
Genealogy and local history resources; small bookstore. Research done by volunteers for modest fee.
• 1007 Main • 253.863.1806
• hqrl.com ❸

A Picket Fence
Accents, gifts, jewelry, accessories like Brighton bags and Tom's shoes. Italian sodas and other confections.
• 1006 Main • 253.863.6048
• apicketfence.com ❹

Sumner Woodworker Store
An eclectic selection of hand and power tools and a changing wood inventory. A bit of a retirement hobby project, the store shows the owners' affection but it's idiosyncratic. That's not always bad.
• 906 Cherry • 253.891.9413 ❺
• sumnerwoodworkerstore.com

Bonney Lake Bicycle Shop
Free bike repair classes, a blog and a wide range of bike types and manufacturers.
• 1406 Main • 253.863.5145
• bonneylakebicycleshop.net ❻

Sumner Motor Inn
An old school motel; free wi fi; pets are welcome; smoking and non-smoking rooms.
• 15506 Main
• 253.863.3250
• sumnermotorinn.com ❼

Sumner Performing Arts Center
The Mane Stage, a nonprofit theatre company, emphasizes family-friendly shows like Oklahoma and Annie. Schedule includes summer shows. • 1707 Main • 253.447.7645
• manestagetheatre.com ❽

The Collectible Cat
Cat-themed gifts and collectibles.
• 923 Kincaid • 253.826.0533
• collectiblecat.lbu.com ❾

Sugar Babies
Tasteful, unique clothes, accessories, and furnishings for little ones and moms-to-be.
• 926 Main, Suite 104
• 253.299.6221
• shopsugarbabies.com ❿

The Simple Kitchen/ Simple Tidings
This established kitchen store features cookbooks, gadgets, cutlery, dishes and decor. ⓫
• 1115 Main, Suite A • 253.863.7933

A Good Book
Old fashioned book store with great staff. New and used; books taken for store credit; ebook access.
• 1014 Main • 253.891.9692 ⓬

Buttered Biscuit
"Authentic Gramma food" with a full bar – Oban neat for Gramma, please - and a gluten-free menu. Biscuits and gravy, prime rib…a big menu. Daily specials, play area.
• 1014 North • 253.826.6099 ⓭

Sorci's Italian Cafe

Great coffee and espresso, gelato, full menu. Outdoor seating, wine bar.
• 1012 Ryan • 253.891.8400
• sorcisitaliancafe.com ⓮

Brank's Barbecue

Kansas City style barbecue since 1995 [meat slow-cooked over wood; sauce is thick, tomato-y and molasses]. The owner co-authored a book for competitive bbq-ers and hosts in-depth classes. Food's good, too. • 13701 24th St. E
• 253.891.1789 ⓯

The Old Cannery Furniture Warehouse

Large furniture store with a few distinctions: peeled log furniture; and – incongruously – a fudge factory.
• 13608 A Valley Ave. E
• 253.863.5484
• oldcanneryfurniture.com ⓰

Berryland Cafe

Opens early; breakfast all day. The staff includes a Giant Berry mascot, which can be unnerving at first. Same friendly owners since 1995. No details on the Giant Berry.
• 1101 Main • 253.863.4567
• berrylandcafe.com ⓱

KC's Caboose

German-inflected railroad diner and bakery. Generous portions.
• 905 Main • 253.863.7273 ⓲

Sabrina's Lunch in a Box

Dine in or take out. Gluten-free bread, pastries and wraps.
• 909 Alder Ave. • 253.987.5402
• sabrinaslunchinabox.net ⓳

The Ryan House Museum

George Ryan was Sumner's first mayor, elected in 1891. This museum depicts his life and times. ⓴
• 1228 Main • 253.299.5780

Reuben H. Knoblaugh Heritage Park

In the heart of downtown, near the commuter railway. Perfect for a picnic lunch, the park also serves as a concert and special event showcase for the city's many festivals and celebrations.
• 914 Kincaid ㉑

Daffodil Valley Sports Complex

Fields, skateboard park, courts and a jogging trail are designed for sports enthusiasts of all ages. Children's play area, picnic spots and concessions.
• 5604 Graham ㉒

For information on city parks: ci.sumner.wa.us/Living/Parks.html

Foothills Trail

The 15-mile Foothills Trail is mostly paved and extends from Meeker to South Prairie Creek, then to a 2-mile trail in Buckley. Walking and biking. ㉓

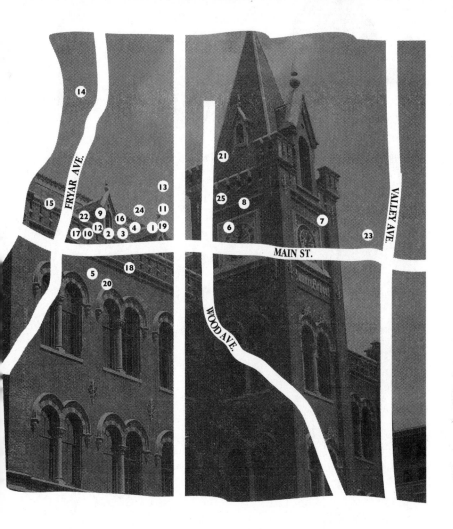

VanLierop Garden Market

Over 70 years old, with an extensive gifts section.

• 1020 Ryan • 253.862.8510
• vanlierops.com ㉔

Windmill Gardens

Retailing since 1982, now featuring bistro and tea shop.

• 16009 60th St. E • 253.863.5843
• windmillgarden.com ㉕

Eatonville

Eatonville is a small town along state route 161 in rural Pierce County. It serves as a gateway to both Mt Rainer National Park and the Gifford Pinchot National Forest. Incorporated in 1901 and long a logging town, Eatonville has become an attraction-filled visitor destination.

L. Lisa Lawrence

Northwest Trek

Donated to the Metro Parks Tacoma in 1971 by Dr. David and Connie Hellyer to serve as a wildlife preserve, Trek is now more than 700 acres, with tram tours featuring free-roaming bison, elk, bighorn sheep and other animals up close. Also on site are nature trails, walking tours and a discovery center.

Staff is knowledgeable and committed to public education. Easily an all-day experience, Trek is unique.
• 11610 Trek Dr. E
• 360.832.6117 • nwtrek.org ❶

Pioneer Farm Museum
Ohop Indian Village
History comes alive at this "hands on" 1887 homestead and a replicated Native American village [seasonal]. Guided tours [about 90 minutes] and over 100 activities provide fun and education for the entire family.
• 7716 Ohop Valley Rd. E
• 360.832.6300
• pioneerfarmmuseum.org ❷

Stringtown Farm and Cellars
This small farm offers the chance to cut lavender in season, shop for plants and lavender products and enjoy hand-crafted wines.
• 9121 Stringtown Rd.
• 360.832.4743
• stringtownfarms.com ❸

Bruno's Restaurant and Bar
The owners' goal: a tail-wagging good time. Named for the family's rescue dog, Bruno's is dog-themed and family friendly. Standard bar menu including burgers, steaks, fish & chips. TVs for sports, Wii for, well, sports also.
• 204 Center • 360.832.7866
• eatbrunos.com ❹

Mountain View Cafe
Burgers from fresh - never frozen - beef, real fruit shakes, hand battered fish and chips as well as over 30 flavors of ice cream make this one of the area's favorite restaurants. • 106 Washington Ave. S
• 360.832.8646 ❺

Eatonville Farmers Market
Locally grown organic fruits and vegetables as well as food specialties and crafts every Saturday, June through September 10AM - 2PM.
• 104 Washington
• 360.879.5535 ❻

Henley's Silver Lake Resort
Set in a beautiful wetlands area featuring rustic cabins, RV and tent camping, duck hunting and fishing from a stocked spring fed lake. Row and paddle boat rentals.
• 40724 S Silver Lake Rd. E
• 360.832.3580
• henleysilverlakeresort.com ❼

Rainbow RV Resort
RV and tent camping, fishing, boat moorage, kitchen and rental on beautiful Tanwax Lake. Camp store and laundry.
• 34217 Tanwax Ct. E
• 360.879.5115
• rainbowrvresort.com ❽

University of Washington
Experimental Pack Forest
4,300 acres of working forest, open to the public for horseback riding, hiking, biking and picnics. Features a conference center and educational forest ecology programs.
• 9010 453rd St. E • 360.832.6534
• packforest.org ❾

Tanwax Greens Golf Course

Nine hole regulation course featuring views of Mt Rainier. This family owned course provides 2,985 yards of golf. Also offers a 12 stall covered driving range.
- 36510 Mountain Hwy. E
- 360.832.8400 ⑩

Eatonville Bird Watching Nature Walks

Weekly guided walks approximately 1.5 miles on Wednesdays and some Saturdays at 10:00 AM viewing waterfowl and wildlife at Smallwood and Mill Pond Parks. Open most months.

Eatonville Outdoor

Bicycles, fishing licenses, skateboards: if it can't be done inside, these folks can help. They've been at it since 2007; in a small town in these times, they're doing something right.
- 101 Mashell Ave. S
- 360.832.2434
- eatonvilleoutdoor.com ⑪

Mountainview Cedar Lodge B & B

This B&B has fabulous mountain views. Remodeling will conclude summer of 2013. Cabins, treehouses and yurts, primitive camping for groups and two RV hookups.
- 36203 Pulford Rd. E
- 360.832.8080 ⑫

Alder Lake Park

This lovely, large lake offers year-round camping, picnicking with ADA- accessible sites, sandy swimming beaches. Boat launches, playgrounds, showers.
- 50324 School Rd. • 360.569.2778
- mytpu.org ⑬

Scale Burger

The area's favorite burger joint, in the nearby town of Elbe on the south end of Alder Lake. Fabulous shakes, outdoor seating.
- 54109 Mountain Hwy. E
- 360.569.2247 ⑭

Copper Creek Inn

Lodge sleeps 12, cabin sleeps five, both creekside in the woods. Conference center. The restaurant, first open in 1946, serves a renowned blackberry pie.
- 35707 State Route 706 E
- 360.569.2799
- coppercreekinn.com ⑮

Mountain Community Co-op

This community hub offers natural and organic foods – there is a difference, but that's for another day – and focuses on local production. A fresh market in season. The Co-op is particularly sensitive to food allergies and stocks products for the lactose- and gluten-intolerant among other specialties.
- 105 Carter • 360.832.2667
- mtncommunitycoop.org ⑯

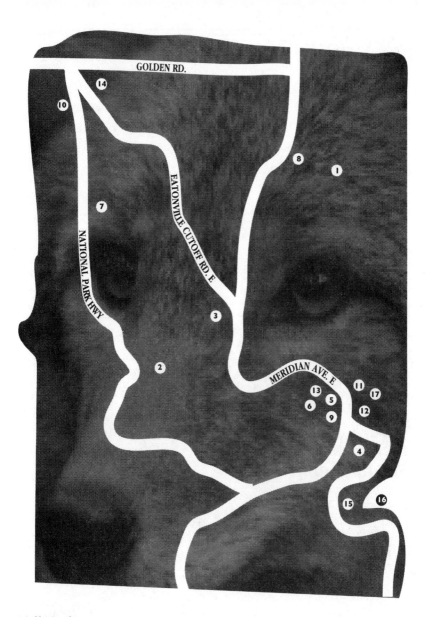

Tall Timber

Most small towns have "the place:" where families go after games, people meet for breakfast before tackling a big job. This is the place in Eatonville. Traditional American food, large portions, reasonable prices, good service.

•121 Mashell •360.832.3535 **17**

Mt. Rainier

Mt Rainier National Park was established in 1899, the fifth park in the system and the first after national forests were separated from the parks. So instead of producing timber, Rainier was the first national resource meant exclusively for recreation and conservation.

Native people considered Rainier – known to them as Takhoma – the most fierce of the four peaks in the Cascade range. [The others are Adams, St Helens and Hood.] This ferocity expressed itself in avalanches, sudden fissures and violent vents of steam and volcanic eruptions with molten flows and flying boulders. And like an old rocker who keeps an amp in the garage, the Mountain hasn't altogether changed its ways. Rainier remains an active volcano, a natural force, awesome in both beauty and destructive power.

The Park has five main areas. They range from well-developed to near-wilderness. Most of the Park is accessible from the South Sound; the small communities along the way are intriguing in themselves.

Brutus Beafcoque

Longmire

Longmire is in the southwest corner of the Park, about seven miles from the Nisqually entrance. Originally Park headquarters, the old lodge is now a museum, with a nearby information center.

The National Park Inn has 25 rooms and a full service restaurant. The gift shop features Native American art and artifacts. The general store – housed in a 1911 log cabin – rents cross-country skis and snowshoes.
• 360.569.2400
• mtrainierguestservices.com

Cougar Rock Campground is about two miles from Longmire. It has 170 individual campsites and five group sites; potable water, toilets and fire grates are all on site. The campground is wooded and just a few hundred feet from the Nisqually River. Reservations are available – and recommended – for this and other campgrounds at recreation. gov.

Longmire is the starting point for several trails and day hikes, some very easy, others more challenging. Within a few miles – on a paved road – are glacier views and a number of waterfalls. One is named Madcap; other names are more mundane.

Paradise

Popular year-round, this is the prime winter-use part of the Park, also accessed from the Nisqually entrance. Paradise is about 12 miles from Longmire along a well-maintained road. At 5,400 feet high, Paradise is the hub for trails to glacial lakes and sub-alpine foliage. Like others in the Park, these are generally well-maintained but vary in difficulty. The altitude is a factor in hikers' endurance and the weather can change fast.

The new Jackson Paradise Visitor Center [closed in winter] has a cafeteria, gift shop and lots of edutainment about the Park.

The Paradise Inn was originally built in 1916 and has 120 guest rooms, a dining room, cafe and gift shop. It too is closed in winter.
• Mtrainierguestservices.com

Though it's best known for vast meadows of wildflowers, Paradise gets a lot of snow in winter and is a popular starting point for snowshoeing and cross-country skiing.

Sunrise

Sunrise – at 6,400 feet the highest point in the Park – is 60 miles from Longmire and about 15 miles from the Sunrise turnoff from Highway 410. It's a short season at Sunrise: late June into September.
There's a visitor center but no overnight lodging; several campsites are

nearby, as are views of glaciers and seemingly close mountain ranges. A fortress and other historic structures are set in the meadows.

Carbon River/Mowich Lake

Easy to reach from State Route 165, this is perhaps the rainiest part of Rainier and in places approximates a temperate rain forest. Because the approach roads are susceptible to wash-out, Mowich is usually open only July – October.

Carbon River offers hiking access to sub-alpine meadows, falls, lakes and glacier views.

Ipsut Creek has backcountry camping [with permit]; it's a five-mile hike from the Carbon River entrance.

Mowich campground is six miles from the Mowich entrance, but driveable.

A few well-marked trails are open, including the short [3/10 mile] Rain Forest Nature Trail near the Carbon River entrance.

Over the past 100 years, communities have grown up near Rainier. Typically started as logging towns, they've come to embrace Park visitors. It's a rough-hewn embrace sometimes, but still...

Enumclaw

A year-round basecamp, with restaurants and cafes, mountain gear including skis, rifles and chainsaws, many places to stay [http://www.enumclawchamber.com/directory/category/innhotel] and nearby trout fishing and hiking.

Wilkeson

About 400 people live here; the town offers off-road RV parking and some stunning old buildings, including an Eastern Orthodox church.

Crystal Mountain

This is a heavily-used ski resort and summer recreation area. Lots of amenities including a lodge, restaurants, equipment rentals and lessons. • staycrystal.com

Greenwater

Just east of Crystal, Greenwater has approximately 67 residents, a few restaurants, equipment sales and rental and idiosyncratic shops.

Elbe

The starting point for the Mt Rainier Scenic Railroad, drawn by a restored steam engine. The MSRR has been running for 25 years for visitors, part of the longest-running steam railroad in the Northwest. • mrsr.com

Dupont

DuPont offers modern conveniences and a terrific touch of history all at the same time. Green spaces, parks, and a series of interconnected trails for walking, running, and biking showcase DuPont's love of the natural environment, while paying homage to the region's earliest settlers. A pristine and welcoming community.

Kim Thompson

DuPont Historic Village

In 1906, the E.I. DuPont de Nemours Company bought over 3,000 acres of land (owned by the Hudson Bay Company) to build a dynamite manufacturing plant. A town was built for the workers that included housing, a park, a clubhouse, stores, and a hotel. In the 1940's the company chose not to own and operate the town and finally DuPont became incorporated in the early 1950's. By 1976, the plant closed but parts of the lovingly preserved historic village remain intact. The tour on foot is an easy walk, just a little over a mile. Parts of the original town buildings and spaces remain to explore.
• 507 Barksdale • 253.964.2399
• visitdupont.com ❶

The DuPont History Museum

The Museum includes the Du-Pont dynamite train and displays on Native American culture, the Hudson Bay Company, DuPont and Weyerhaeuser. Gift shop. Admission is free; donations are welcome.
• 207 Barksdale • 253.964.2399
• dupontmuseum.com

Parks and Trails

DuPont prides itself on parks and trails. Easily accessible, the trail system consists of paved walkways and dirt/gravel trails, interspersed with twelve parks. The city boasts 50 acres of parks and 12 miles of designated trails and bike lanes, including access to historical sites, lush native plants and greenery and terrific views. Some trails are flat and easy and others are more sloping and moderate. • 253.576.0696
• visitdupont.com

The Home Course

This lovely course hosted the first days of play in the 2010 U.S. Amateur Open. Some holes have glimpses of the South Sound. Lessons, range, and golf specials are available. • 2300 Golf House Rd.
• 866.964.0520
• thehomecourse.com ❸

Eagles Pride Golf Course

An award-winning military golf course, located on JBLM. Here's the good news: it's open to the general public. Practice range and golf specials. Prepare for security check at the Main Gate.
• I-5 Exit 116 JBLM, Lewis Main Gate
• 253.967.6522 • jblmmwr.com ❹

GuestHouse Inn and Suites DuPont

Great views of Mt. Rainier or the Home Course. Centrally located to local sights, JBLM, Olympia, and Tacoma.
• 1609 McNeil St. • 800.214.8378
• visitdupont.com/hotels ❺

The Liberty Inn at DuPont Station

This hotel, just steps from businesses and eateries, is a comfortable spot for business and vacation travelers. • 1400 Wilmington Dr.
• 253.912.8777 ❻

McNamara's Pub and Eatery

This family owned restaurant has served the community for 30 years offering American cuisine with an Irish twist. • 1595 Wilmington Dr.
• 253.964.9200 ❼

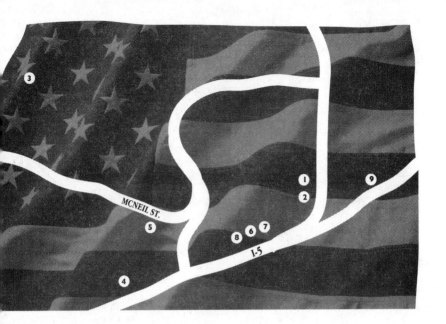

The Fortune Cookie

This restaurant serves up Chinese and Thai cuisine in a great central location in town. • 1575 Wilmington Dr. • 253.964.9357 ❽

Fort Lewis Military Museum

A good resource for researchers as well as intriguing displays of uniforms, arms and transportation. Gift shop. Visitors should obtain passes at the Main Gate Visitors Center; pass requires identification, vehicle insurance and registration.
• 253.967.4523
• fortlewismuseum.com ❾

Steilacoom

Tucked along the edge of Puget Sound, Steilacoom was the first incorporated town (1854) in Washington Territory. Commanding views of Puget Sound. Buildings and sites on the National Registry of Historic Places. Beaches, parks, and museums. Old fashioned ice cream soda or a glass of wine at one of the unique local restaurants.

Carolyn Burt

Bair Drug and Hardware Store

Bair's maintains the original working 1908 soda fountain amidst turn of the century furnishings including post office boxes, hardware, bottles. Open for breakfast, lunch and dinner. • 1617 Lafayette
• 253.584.4133 ❶

Historic Houses/Monuments

Over 30 houses and monuments in Steilacoom are on the National Register of Historic Sites. A "Touring Map" is available at Bair Drug or the Steilacoom Historical Museum.
• steilacoomhistorical.org

Chambers Creek Fish Trap

September through March, salmon return to the fish ladder to spawn in Chamber's Creek . Great place to see geese, ducks, blue heron and resident bald eagles. Northwest end of Chambers Creek Rd. W ❷

Sunnyside Beach

Saltwater shoreline provides areas for dog walking, kayak launch, volleyball, beachcombing, outdoor shower, covered picnic area, BBQ, restrooms, geographical signs, and children's play area. • Chamber's Creek Rd. W • 253.581.1912 ❸

Farrell's Marsh

Great for bird watching. Walking trails wind through a forested area to a wetland pond, three view points and a log foot bridge.
• Chambers Ct. and Beech Ave.
• 253.581.1912 ④

Orchard Pioneer Park

The old-fashioned glider swing offers the best views of Puget Sound! Geographical signs identify mountains and islands. The Robert W. Anderson Jr. Bandstand is a popular place for photos. ⑤
• Intersection of Commercial and Wilkes • 253.581.1912

Saltar's Point Park

Saltwater shoreline, picnic facilities. Marine sanctuary: diving is permitted. Besides shipwrecked boats, one may see rockfish, lingcod, sculpin, painted greenlings, gunnels, and crab. Check the Washington Department of Fish and Wildlife for details.
• 1st St. and Champion
• 253.581.1912 ⑥

Byrd Mill Park

Monument commemorates the only escape route from the Puyallup Valley to Fort Steilacoom during the Indian War of 1855. Site of the Russian American Telegraph Line. Picnic area. • Corner of Lafayette and Union. ⑦

Chamber's Creek Canyon Park and Trail

Some rough and steep trails along a deep ravine. Trails go down to Chamber's Creek. Haven to forest birds, deer, coyote, and native plants. Near fish ladder on the right, pullout and trailhead sign. Limited parking. • Chambers Creek Rd.
• 253.798.4177 ⑧

Charles R. Buchanan Park AKA Charlie's Park

Tiered deck park offers views of ferry boats, islands, Olympic Mountains and wildlife. Geographical signs and benches. Geocachers will find a cache here as well as others scattered throughout the town.
• Pacific between Layfayette and Commercial. ⑨

Parks

Steilacoom has several other parks with such amenities as picnic tables, basketball and tennis courts, and jungle gyms. • 253.581.1912
• townofsteilacoom.com

La Creme Brulee Cafe et Bistro Francais

Authentic French cuisine and charming atmosphere. Lunch on Thursday and Friday from 12- 2 p.m. Dinner from 5:30 p.m. to closing on Wednesday, Thursday, Friday, and Saturday. Reservations encouraged. • 1606 Lafayette
• 253.589.3001
• lacremebrulee.com ⑩

Topside Bar and Grill

A good spot for a glass of wine or to watch the sunset. Lunch and dinner; no sunsets at lunch. Variety of menu items but known for fish and chips. All year outer deck seating.
• 215 Wilkes
• 253.212.3690 ⓫

Two Teaspoons Cafe

For a latte and a small snack; downstairs from the Topside.
• 215 Wilkes • 253.292.0431 ⓬

Espresso by the Bay

Coffee to go at the drive in window, seating inside.
• 1203 Rainier • 253.581.1657 ⓭

Steilacoom Pub and Grill

Karaoke Friday and Saturday nights; trivia, open mic, pool. A good pub menu.
• 1202 Rainier • 253.584.7693
• thesteilacoompubandgrill.com ⓮

Concerts in the Park

Every Wednesday at 6:30 p.m. during June, July and August. Each year features a series of free public concerts at the Bandstand in Pioneer Orchard Park. • Check www.steilacoom.org for a list of the concerts. • Intersection of Wilkes and Commercial Streets.

Ferry Dock and Boat Launch

Terminal for Ketron and Anderson Islands and boat to McNeil Island Penitentiary. Clyde V. Davidson Fishing Pier. Fishing and crabbing free for under 15 years of age; permit needed for adults. Public boat launch. • West end of Union and Commercial. ⓯

Inn at Saltars Point

Two spacious French Country style private suites with panoramic views of Puget Sound. Saltar's Point Beach, a protected marine habitat, just a five minute walk. Bicycles included. • 86 Jackson
• 253.588.4522
• innatsaltarspoint.com ⓰

Above the Sound Bed and Breakfast

Ground level guest suite, home-like setting, private backyard and garden. Full or continental breakfasts available. Walking distance to town.
• 806 Birch
• 253.589.1441 ⓱

Farmers' Market

Wednesdays 3-7 p.m. June, July, and August. Fresh produce, baked goods, cheeses, handcrafted glass, flowers, crafts and specialty items. Located on the multi-purpose tennis courts next to the Steilacoom Town Hall. • Corner of Lafayette and Wilkes

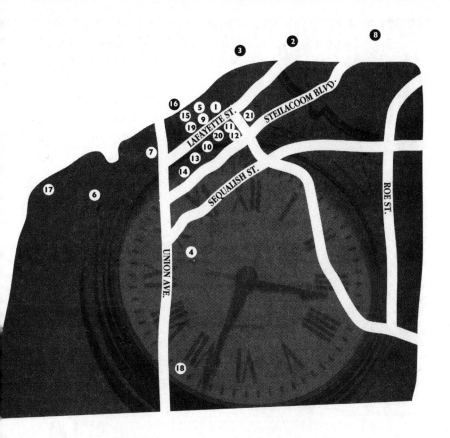

Steilacoom Tribal Museum and Cultural Center

Baskets, tools, traditional clothing, crafts, photos, and artifacts dating back to the 1400s. The gift shop features Native handcrafted items. Open Saturdays from 10 a.m. - 4 p.m. Small entry fee. Tours available. • 1515 Lafayette • 253.584.6308 ⑱

Steilacoom Historical Museum

Photos and artifacts from the town's historic past. Guide to the historic sites. Entry to the museum, Wagon shop, and Orr Home: $2 donation. Weekends and Wednesdays in summer. • 1801 Rainier • 253.588.3591 or 253.584.4133 ⑲

The Wagon Shop

Contains many of Nathaniel Orr's tools, wood-working equipment, forge as well as a buggy, sleigh and farm cart. Open during special events, by request during normal Steilacoom Historical Museum hours or by appointment. • Main Street between Rainier and Lafayette. • 253.565.5350 ⑳

The Nathaniel Orr Home and Orchard

Open when the Steilacoom Historical Museum is open. Restored to include original furniture dating from 1868. • 1811 Rainier • 253.588.3591 • steilacoomhistorical.org ㉑

Anderson Island

How can a small historic island in the South Puget Sound transform visitors and capture their imaginations? Witness Anderson Island. Only a short ferry ride from Steilacoom, this island gem offers tranquility and natural beauty like no other. Whether for an easy day trip or a weekend holiday, this is a perfect showcase for the Sound.

Anderson Island prides itself on parks and trails and it should. Visitors can explore lush forest, beautiful wetlands and long stretches of shoreline boasting incredible maritime views. Birdwatchers are in for a real treat; the island boasts many species, notably bald eagle and heron. And beachcombing is great fun and can yield close-up views of orcas, pods of porpoise or seals.

Kim Thompson

Andy's Marine Park

This 81-acre park offers terrific hiking trails through native plants and trees. The trail works its way to the shoreline and the views are spectacular. Good shoes and water to drink are recommended. This trail does have some steep inclines. Clausen Road (website below for directions). ❶

Andy's Wildlife Park

Nearly 200 acres in size, this park has forest, tidal estuaries and wetlands. The main trail is a nicely paced two mile stroll (the hike is most enjoyable during the warmer months due to drier trail conditions). Adjacent is a fenced dog park. • Eckenstam-Johnson Rd. ❷

For information about these parks and other featured parks on the island: • *253.884.2110* • *andersonislandparks.org*

Johnson Farm

Established in 1896 by early Anderson Island settlers. The farm is the home of the Anderson Island Historical Society, which has lovingly maintained period buildings, farm equipment, furnishings and heirlooms. Museum and gift shop on the property as well as a large, lush community garden.
• 9306 Otso Point Rd.
• andersonislandhs.org ❸

Riviera Community Club and Lakeshore Restaurant

This homeowner's association is nestled near an excellent golf course and restaurant. While these amenities are for residents, guests are welcome. • 11016 Country Club Dr. • 253.884.4093 and 253.884.3344 • rivieraclub.org ❹

Frick, Frack and Frillie Coffee Shop

This quaint shop is an island mainstay. Tasty hot and cold beverages, breakfast and lunch menus and grab 'n' go goodies make this restaurant a hit with locals and visitors.
• 10202 Eckenstam-Johnson Rd.
• 253.884.1644 ❺

Island General Store

This is the ONLY store on Anderson Island. Besides groceries, the store features an award winning deli, DVD rental, post office, gas and propane services, a ferry ticket kiosk and more.
• 10202 Eckenstan-Johnson Rd.
• 253.884.4001 ❻
• andersonislandgeneralstore.com

The Island doesn't have hotels but does have charming and convenient bed and breakfast options.

Annabelle's Bed and Breakfast

One suite in a separate building with balcony. Private beach.
• 13016 134th Ave. • 253.884.1095
• annabellesbandb.com ❼

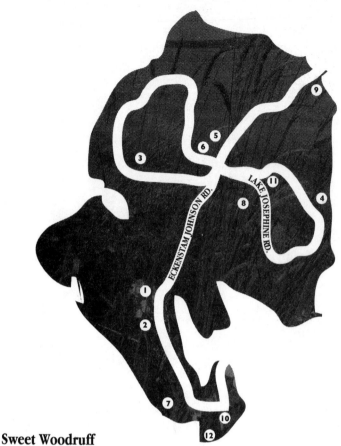

Sweet Woodruff
Bed and Breakfast

Suite with private bath in a forest setting. Sweet. 10717 Olympic Pl. •253.884.2180 • sweetwoodruffbedandbreakfast.com ❽

Inn at Burg's Landing

A rustic log building with two guest rooms, one a master suite. Private beach. •8808 Villa Beach Rd. •253.884.9185 •burgslandingbb.com ❾

August Inn

Terrific waterfront setting. Three distinct units; the main building sleeps six in 1,300 square feet; the two smaller units are one-bedrooms and sleep two each. All the units are self-contained. No pets; no smoking inside the units. • 14117 Lyle Point Rd. • 253.884.4011 •augustinn.com ❿

Bond's Lake Chalet

Facing Lake Josephine, adjacent to playfield including tennis courts. Canoe available. One unit. •10411 Narrows Dr. •253.884.9655 ⓫

Anderson Island Kayaks

Gear rental, basic instruction, tours. Kids okay with an adult. All weather; reservations recommended. • 12106 144th St. • 253.884.6911 • andersonislandkayaks.com ⓬

Fircrest

Established in 1925 to be an "enchanting community," Fircrest has largely succeeded. Local businesses are surrounded by cozy homes and lush parks, close to larger cities. As locals know, traffic laws are strictly enforced.

Jackie Fender

Fircrest Tot Lot

An enclosed playground with slides, swings, teeter totters and sandbox. Popular spot for play dates. By this we mean children's play dates.
• 5th and Contra Costa ❶

The Greener Bean

Welcoming spot for coffee or loose leaf tea, whether working or relaxing. Warm ambiance, Wi-Fi, house-made pastries and meaty panini.
• 1039 Regents Blvd.
• 253.564.7336
• greenerbeancoffee.com ❷

Innovative Fitness

Gain or maintain physical well being with one-on-one training at Innovative Fitness. Quality equipment and nutritional support available whether working on a regime or just dropping in for a workout.
• 1105 Regents Blvd.
• 253.565.1965 ❸

Fircrest Pool/ Community Center

Fircrest Community Center hosts community events and can be booked for private gatherings. The outdoor pool is open from Memorial Day until Labor Day. • 555 Contra Costa Avenue
• 253.564.8177 • cityoffircrest.net ❹

121

Fircrest Park

More play? Fircrest Park has a playground, gazebo and picnic space. •471 Electron Way ❺

Day Spa Adriana

Spa and massage services. Appointments recommended. •2079 Mildred Street W •253.778.0980 ❻

Viafore's Italian Delicatessen

An area staple with a classic deli feel. Cold and hot sandwiches to eat in or take out; pasta dishes include manicotti and lasagna. Order ahead for large quantities. •604 Regents Blvd •253.564.2228 ❼

Fircrest Swim Shop

Distinctive selection of suits and other gear, with an emphasis on competitive swimming. •620 Regents Blvd. •253.565.9615 ❽

Thelma Gilmur Park

Seven serene acres named for a local environmental activist. Walking trails, varied foliage and wildlife. •40th and Emerson ❾

Christopher Columbus Bocce Courts

Three public courts, crushed rock surface. •Corner of Contra Costa and Elm Tree. ❿

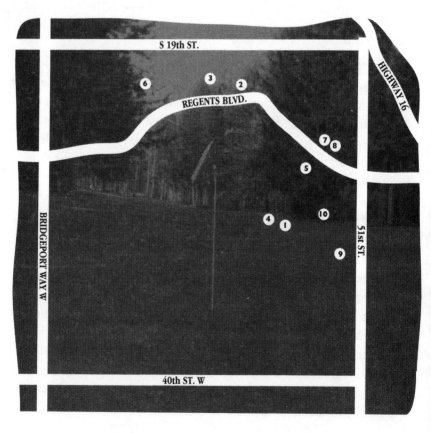

University Place & Chambers Bay

University Place (UP) is a vibrant young city incorporated in 1995. UP has a healthy community feel with clean, safe streets, excellent schools, and enthusiastic volunteers for sports, arts, gardening, parks, and family-centered parades and celebrations. Situated on Puget Sound, many parts of UP enjoy views of Mt. Rainier, the Olympic Mountains or the Narrows Bridge.

Carmen Sterba

Chambers Bay Golf Course

Like other sports - running the marathon in ancient Greece or kayaking for whale in the Arctic - golf began in nature. As early as the 15th century golfers at Scotland's St Andrews trenched thru sand dunes to place holes where the terrain allowed. [We won't debate whether golf really began in Scotland, in Holland or in China; reasonable people disagree, as do golfers.]

Because St Andrews is in an area called the Linksland, its type of course is called "links." Links courses are on or near a major body of water, which in turn means sand dunes and routinely irregular winds. Links courses have few trees or on-course hazards. The U.S. Open is always played on a links course.

Chambers Bay is set on a 930 acre site owned by Pierce County. At its core the property is a water treatment facility, cleaning flow from across the county before the water reaches Puget Sound. Above ground the property is covered with trails and parkland and an environmental learning center.

And one of the finest public golf courses in the world.

Driven by the vision of then-executive John Ladenburg, Pierce County commissioned course architect Robert Trent Jones II to create a links experience true to the game's legacy and the challenging bay-side terrain. Construction started in 2005; the course opened two years later. Since then Chambers Bay has been named the country's second best municipal course [Golfweek] and hosted the 2010 U.S. Amateur Championship.

In 2015 Chambers Bay will host the U.S. Open, joining courses like Pebble Beach, Pinehurst, Winged Foot and Torrey Pines and focusing global attention on the dunes, that solitary pine tree and the stunning Puget Sound.

The course is open May thru November; rates vary by season and by time of day. Players have unlimited use of the practice facility; group rates and season passes available. • 6320 Grandview W • 877.29.LINKS • chambersbaygolf.com ❶

Chambers Bay Bike and Hike Trail

A 3.25-mile loop of flat ground and hills encircles the golf course and extends to the Bridge to the Beach for access to the Puget Sound. • 6320 Grandview Dr. ❷

Curran Orchard Resource Enthusiasts

CORE holds pruning parties, classes, tours, summer concerts (June-Aug), and an annual cider squeeze. • Meetings the 1st Wed. at 7 pm. • curranappleorchard.com

SUNdogs

The group maintains the off-leash dog park at Chambers Bay, holds events like Santa Paws pet photos and meets 3rd Wed. at 7 pm. • updogpark.org

UP Community Garden

Citizen gardeners donate time or part of their plot to the local food bank. Located at the intersection of 40th St. W and 67th St. W • upcommuntygarden.org

UP for Arts

This arts group has procured unique sculptures around the city, such as Georgia Gerber's bronze duck, and organizes spring and summer concert series.
• upforart.org

Ducks also feature prominently in such events as the Duck Parade, Duck Daze and Duck the Halls. Information at the main pond, cityofup.com

Knutsen's Northwest Sportscards

At Green Firs Shopping Center; includes gaming cards, gaming tournaments, and packwars.
• 3816 Bridgeport Way
• 253.564.9204
• nw-sportscards.com ❸

Northwest Snowboards & Skateboards

A well-informed and friendly staff and reasonable prices. • 2805 Bridgeport Way • 253.564.5974
• nwsnowboards.com ❹

Adriana Hess Wetlands Park and Audubon Center

A partnership among Tahoma Audubon Society, Audubon Washington and UP Parks. Plant walks and bird walks on 2 acres of native plants and trees, trails, wetlands, a pond and gift shop.
• 2917 Morrison Rd. • 253.565.9278
• wa.audubon.org ❺

Cirque Park

Located one-half block east of 40th and Bridgeport, where UP Parks holds baseball, softball & t-ball games. ❻

The Sharing by John Jewell

Sculpture located at 7250 Cirque Dr. W

Colgate Park

This small space-themed park is good for picnics and for its playground. • 3717 Grandview Dr.
• 253.566.5656 • cityofup.com ❼

Homestead Park

Blooms in spring with hundreds of daffodils and rhododendrons. Within the park is The Slug sculpture by Christopher Hoppi. Annual flower show here. • 3761 Bridgeport Way ❽

Affairs Cafe and Bakery

A congenial place for breakfast or lunch and take out; homemade gourmet chocolates and desserts.
• 2811 Bridgeport Way W Suite 15
• 253.565.8504 ❾

Chambers Bay Grill

The grill and bar attached to the Chambers Bay golf course and hiking trail. The food gets raves. •6320 Grandview Dr. W •253.460.4653 ⑩

Chili Thai Restaurant

Friendly atmosphere with soft music, varied menu. •7406 27th St. W •253.564.9099 •chilithai.com ⑪

El Toro

A family-friendly atmosphere; in Green Fir Shopping Center. •3820 Bridgeport Way W ⑫ •253.565.2265 •eltorofamily.com

Frog 'n Kiwi Cafe

Healthy food and drinks; play center for children. •Located by the library in the Civic Building at 3609 Market Place W •253.617.1434 ⑬

Green Spot Tea House and Art Gallery

A friendly hideaway for specialty teas and healthy food. Local art on sale. •3318 Bridgeport Way ⑭ •253.565.2832 •greenspottea.com

Herfy Burgers

Tasty and original burgers. Dine in or take out at the corner of Cirque (56th) and Orchard. •5510 Orchard St. W #B3 •253.474.2411 ⑮

India Mahal Restaurant

Plentiful lunch buffet in a soothing atmosphere. •1905 Bridgeport Way •253.564.2039 •indiamahal.com ⑯

Jade Palace

Chinese restaurant & lounge for 35 years; recently received the News Tribune's Golden Fork Award. •3318 Bridgeport Way •253.564.7170 ⑰

Lefty's Burger Shack

Distinguished by the surfer guy billboard and retro '50s style; best burgers in UP. Take out only. •8317 27th St. W •253.565.0887 ⑱

Miyoshi Japanese Restaurant

Sushi and various Japanese-style cooked dishes. •2310 Mildred St. W Suite 102 •253.565.0738 ⑲

Pine Cone Cafe

A neighborhood family restaurant since 1950 with a nostalgia-inducing menu; great breakfasts. •7912 27th St. W •253.565.5690 ⑳

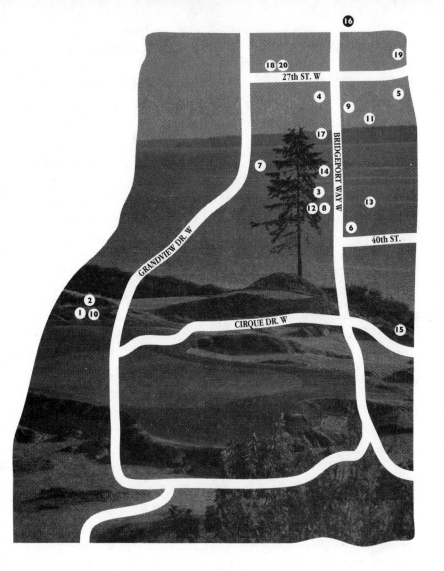

Lakewood

Lakewood is rightly proud of its community spirit, diverse culture and modern infrastructure. Well-kept parks, sparkling lakes, historic sites and global amenities add to the city's appeal. With multiple access points and location between Olympia and Tacoma, Lakewood is convenient to visit and primed for growth.

Kim Thompson

Lakewold Gardens
Ten tranquil acres of rare and native plants and trees (nearly 1,000 rhododendrons alone) and terrific views of Gravelly Lake and Mt. Rainer. Once owned by the Hudson's Bay Company, the estate was established in 1910. The in-tact Georgian style mansion is an historic landmark.
12317 Gravelly Lake Dr. SW ❶
253.584.4106 lakewoldgardens.org

Lakewood History Museum
Documents, maps, and artifacts from early geologic time [not many documents from this period], Native American life and European settlement. Also host to traveling exhibits. Admission free, donations welcome.
• 6211 Mt Tacoma Dr. SW
• 253.682.3480
• lakewoodhistorical.org ❷

Ft. Steilacoom Park

The largest park in Lakewood, its 340 acres include extensive trails, multiple sports fields, a spectacular children's playground, dog park (segregated for smaller and larger breeds) and picnic facilities (covered and uncovered). •8714 87th Ave. SW ❸

American Lake Park

Beach front, swimming, playgrounds, boat launch. •9222 Veterans Dr. SW • cityoflakewood.us ❹

International District

This district, shared with Tacoma, is located on South Tacoma Way between 80th and 96th Streets. Besides goods and services, there are many ethnic restaurants and shopping. ❺

Paldo World

A shopping center with Korean market, cosmetics store and gift shop including a French bakery/restaurant; signage in Korean and English with bi-lingual staff. •9601 S. Tacoma Way • 253.581.7800 ❻

Boo Han International Village

Asian [emphasizing Korean] and American foods in the cornerstone supermarket expanding to 1 million sq. ft. in early 2013. Offers a wide variety of imported foods, household goods, produce, specialty meat items and a deli department with freshly made items including Korean sushi, fried dried squid

and acorn starch jelly. •9122 So. Tacoma Way • 253.588.7300 ❼

Carr's Restaurant & Bar

A family friendly restaurant offering American fare, catering, and orders to go. • 11006 Bridgeport Way SW •253.584.4622
• carrsrestaurant.net ❽

Moonrise Cafe

Traditional American cuisine with vegetarian and vegan options. ❾
•6020 Main St. SW • 253.983.9999

Stina's Cellars Winery

Offering a variety of quality, affordable wines produced in small lots. Limited hours but worth checking. •9316 Lakeview Avenue
• 253.227.9748 • stinacellars.com ❿

French Hen Bistro

An eclectic lunch/dinner menu. The Bistro specializes in truffles; good decision. •3810 Steilacoom Blvd. SW • 253.983.1313
• frenchhenbistro.com ⓫

Thornewood Castle

Built 100 years ago with bricks shipped from Wales, Thornewood is available for vacation rental or B&B stay; it's among the premier accomodations in the Northwest. The lake-front grounds offer forest, beach and English gardens. Furnishings and artwork have been lovingly preserved. •8601 N Thorne Ln. SW
• 253.584.4393
• thornewoodcastle.com ⓬

Fort Steilacoom Golf Course

An accessible nine hole public course adjacent to beautiful Fort Steilacoom Park. •8200 87th Ave. SW •253.588.0613 •lakespanawaygc.com ⓭

Lakewood State Game Refuge

90 acres under state management, set aside in 1922 for conservation and education. Current restoration is focused on oak-woodland prairie habitat. Birds, including raptors, deer and small mammals and reptiles. •7801 Phillips Rd. SW •wdfw.wa.gov ⓮

Steeped in Comfort

A traditional tea room with salads, sandwiches, pastries and High Tea. Stationery and gifts are also on offer. •11016 Gravelly Lake Dr. SW •253.582.1336 •steepedincomfort.com ⓯

Tactical Tailor

One of the country's leading manufacturers of combat and law enforcement gear: holsters, vests and armor…serious stuff. This is equipment troops and police buy for themselves, because it's often better than standard issue. •Retail store located at 12715 Pacific Highway South West •866.984.7854, ext 298 •tacticaltailor.com ⓰

House of Donuts

The News Tribune's Sue Kidd calls this Doughnut Mecca; donut lovers rave. One of the machines made pastry for the 1962 Seattle World's Fair. The building is a little triangle, the sign – an old-school vertical neon reading, yes, DONUTS – is frequently photographed. •9638 Gravelly Lake Dr. •253.588.2647 ⓱

Lakewood Costumes

For the usual – or unusual – costume needs; same place, same owner for over 30 years. On-site face-painting and clowning classes. •5932 Lake Grove St. SW •253. 588.6062 •clownshop.com ⓲

Swan's Candles

Beeswax, encaustic art supplies, aromatic oils, wicks, color chips; wholesale and retail. Free classes. •8933 Gravelly Lake Dr. •253.584.4666 •swanscandles.com ⓳

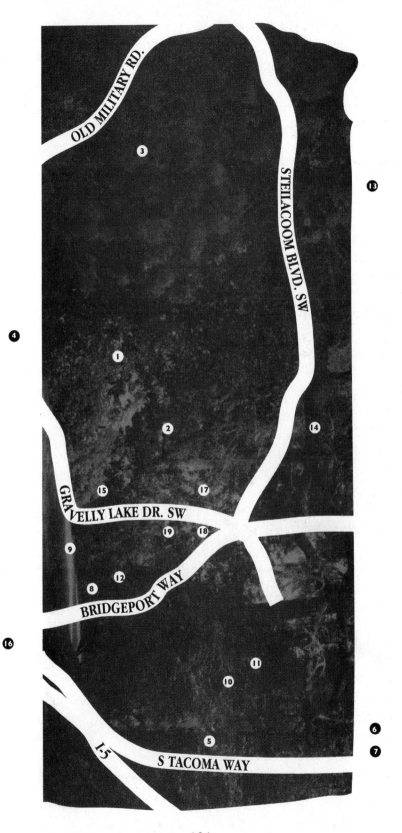

▲▲▲

PART TWO:
THURSTON COUNTY

Downtown Olympia

With unique shops, bars and restaurants, this neighborhood epitomizes downtowns before malls and suburbs; everything is within walking distance of Sylvester Park, the state capital campus, the fountain on 4th Avenue (a children's favorite) and the new City Hall. Not everything's scrubbed and gleaming but all of it's real.

Alec Clayton

Matter Gallery

This colorful art gallery near Capital Lake is crammed with art, crafts and furnishings by more than 100 artists, mostly regional, and all made from recycled materials. Lamps, jewelry, wall hangings, sculpture; there's a little bit of everything.
• 113 Fifth Ave. SW • 360.943.1760
• matteroly.com ❶

Childhood's End Gallery

A combination gift shop and art gallery with one-of-a-kind handcrafted items: glassware to jewelry to woodwork. Gallery exhibits rotate monthly and feature local artists.
• 222 4th Ave. W
• 360.943.3724
• childhoods-end-gallery.com ❷

Rebecca Howard Mural

The new mural on the south side of The Bread Peddler honors Olympia pioneer Rebecca Howard, an African-American woman who with her husband built the Pacific House hotel and restaurant in downtown Olympia in 1859.
• 222 N Capitol Way

The Olympia-Rafah Sister City Mural

This 4,000 square-foot mural honors Rachel Corrie, killed in Palestine while protecting a home from demolition. Approximately 150 participants painted the hundreds of olive leaves; each leaf tells a story. Corner of State and Capitol • olympiarafahmural.org

Washington Center for the Performing Arts

With a four-level, 983-seat proscenium theater plus a "black box," the Washington Center is the largest performance space in Southwest Washington. Traveling shows range from symphonies to jazz, dance and theatre to comedy and lectures.
• 512 Washington St. • 360.753.8585
• washingtoncenter.org ❸

Wind Up Here

To call it a toy store would be a gross understatement. Wind Up Here is a play and learning adventure. Puzzles, games, arts and miscellaneous brain stumpers for all. • 121 5th Ave. SE • 360.943.9045
• winduphere.com ❹

Harlequin Productions

Top-notch professional theatre with local actors in the revamped State Theater; specializing in cutting-edge drama and comedy; Shakespeare and a rock and roll music review every summer.
• 202 4th Ave. E • 360.786.0151
• harlequinproductions.org ❻

The Bread Peddler

Delightful breads, some made only from "wild" yeasts in the air, all from organic ingredients. Coffee, pastries and cafe food. Since 2006 an established meeting spot for Olympia's varied communities.
• 222 Capitol Way N • 360.352.1175
• breadpeddler.com

Capital Playhouse

This local theater hosts musicals for and by adults and children. An Olympia institution since 1986, the black box theater typically features a combination of professional and amateur actors and directors.
• 612 Fourth Ave. E • 360.943.2744
• capitalplayhouse.com ❼

Capitol Theater

The old Capitol Theater is home to the Olympia Film Society and features second-runs, art films and musical concerts. Popcorn sacks are filled halfway, patrons add their own condiments, then the sack is filled. • 206 5th Ave. SE
• 360.754.6670
• olympiafilmsociety.org ❽

Archibald Sisters

This eclectic little shop is the place for pampering with fragrances, body wash, oils and lotions for men and women; massage therapists on duty.
• 406 Capitol Way S • 360.943.2707
• archibaldsisters.com ❾

Compass Rose

Retail is theatre here. The offerings are heavy to indie products including decor, accessories, baby gear, cards and kitchen tools. Like chefs cooking with what's fresh, these folks bring in small batches of tasteful goods. • 416 Capitol Way S
• 360.236.0788
• compassroseolympia.com ❿

The Urban Onion

A bar and restaurant in the old Olympia Hotel, spacious and surprisingly quiet. It's where the Olympia LGBT community meets and greets. The hummus tray is a meal for two, and the fried sweet potatoes complement any dish.
• 116 Legion Way • 360.943.9242
• theurbanonion.com ⓫

Darby's Cafe

It's tiny and crowded and the waits are long, but the atmosphere and decor are funky fun, and so is the menu. Portions are enormous and there are vegan and vegetarian selections. Wizard of Oz memorabilia: always in good taste. • 211 5th Ave. SE • 360.357.6229
• darbyscafe.com ⓬

The Brotherhood Lounge

In the heart of Olympia's downtown core, the Brotherhood is one the most popular bars among the young and hip and the aspiring. There are movie nights, bands, many special events, and the fenced smoking lounge out the back door is one of the largest and often most crowded in town. • 119 Capitol Way N • 360.352.4153
• thebrotherhoodlounge.com ⓭

The 4th Avenue Tavern

Loud and raucous with live music, five pool tables, air hockey, video games, a full kitchen and a large back room for dancing (total seating capacity 400-plus) the 4th Avenue Tavern is a happening place on a happening avenue.
• 210 4th Ave. E • 360.786.1444
• the4thave.com ⓮

Last Word Books

Much larger than it looks from the outside, Last Word Books has ceiling-to-floor shelves jammed with mostly used books, and an in-house press for printing and publishing.
• 211 4th Ave. E • 360.786.WORD
• lastwordbooks.org ⓯

Orca Books

Henry the store cat welcomes browsers to Olympia's oldest and largest independent bookstore. New and used books; local and regional authors strongly supported.
• 509 4th Ave. E • 360.352.0123
• orcabooks.com ⓰

Hands On Children's Museum

It's all hands-on at the children's museum where kids learn about art and science by doing. They can build scale-model cargo ships and a working waterfront, care for the orphaned and injured animals in the Wildlife Rescue Center and much more. 106 11th Ave SW (The museum will move into its new home at the Port of Olympia at Jefferson Street and Olympia Avenue in fall 2012)
•360.956.0818 •hocm.org **17**

Fish Brewing and Fishtale Brew Pub

Part of the first wave of Northwest craft brewers; the Pub goes way past the standards; free wi-fi.
•515 Jefferson SE •360.943.6480
•fishbrewing.com **18**

Spar Cafe

An Olympia classic, now part of the McMenamin's group. Gorgeous interior, super breakfast, the usual tavern menu taken up a notch; kids menu; micro-brew ales on tap.
•114 4th Ave. E •360.357.6444
•McMenamins.com **19**

Canvas Works

One of the region's best fabric retailers; extensive knitting goods as well as fabric for apparel, quilting, upholstery and outdoor use. Classes, equipment.
- 525 Columbia SW • 360.352.4481
- canvasworks.net ⓴

The Mark

Perhaps Olympia's best restaurant, and one of the top spots in the South Sound. Rustic Tuscan, certified organic, moderate pricing. Chef Lisa Owen is a former Berkeley foodie who moved to Rome and then Florence, studying film, architecture and finally food. She renovated a 1940s tire warehouse in 2001; not even the squid is rubbery now. Family friendly; full bar.
- 407 Columbia St. • 360.754.4414
- themarkolympia.com ㉑

Bayside Quilting

Fabric, rotating displays of traditional and contemporary quilts, supplies and machines and classes.
- 225 State Ave. NE • 360.357.2000 baysidequilting.com ㉒

New Moon Cafe

Excellent breakfast spot with lots of vegetarian options including Tofu Benedict. Lunch too. Kids menu.
- 113 4th Ave. W • 360.357.3452
- newmooncafeolympia.com ㉓

Governor Hotel

Great location, complimentary breakfast and wi-fi.
- 621 S Capitol Way
- 360.352.7700
- olywagov.com/hotel ㉔

Capital Campus

One of the South Sound's loveliest views: the sun setting behind the Capitol dome. But that iconic image is just the beginning of the glories of the Capital Campus — located just south of downtown — and its surroundings, including the South Capital neighborhood, filled with lovely homes from the early 20th century.

Molly Gilmore

Legislative Building

Boasting a 278-foot-tall dome, the building has won the praise of architecture critics. It's open to the public daily; free hour-long tours begin at the information desk just inside the main entrance. • 416 Sid Snyder Ave. SW • 360.902.8881 • wa.gov/visitor

Governor's Mansion

The oldest building on the campus, the Georgian-style mansion has been home to the state's governors since 1909. It's furnished with antiques and features a changing art exhibit as well as a portrait of George Washington painted in 1850 by Rembrandt Peale. The mansion also boasts a panoramic view of the city, the Capital grounds, Puget Sound and the Olympic Mountains. Tours of the mansion Wednesdays by reservation.
• wagovmansion.org

Temple of Justice

The appropriately named temple, fronted by sandstone columns, houses the State Supreme Court and Law Library. It's open to the public. Law buffs can call or look online to find out when the Supreme Court is in session.
• 415 12th Ave. SW • 360.902.8881 or 360.357.2077 • courts.wa.gov

War Memorials

The campus boasts six war memorials and another in honor of law-enforcement officers who died in the line of duty. Winged Victory, the World War I monument, features a 12-foot-tall statue of Nike of Samothrace, the Greek goddess of victory, as well as figures of a sailor, a soldier, a marine and a Red Cross nurse. Brochures about the memorials are available at the information desk in the Legislative Building.

Other Sculptures

A more eclectic selection of art can be found to the east of Capitol Way. Among the pieces are James Lee Hansen's The Shaman, an abstract bronze depicting a prehistoric Native American medicine man, and Thomas Jay's Boiler Works, a nine-piece steel and bronze sculptural work inspired by ancient landscapes and meant to encourage interaction.

Tivoli Fountain

Probably the best-known piece of art on the campus is the fountain, easily visible from Capitol Way. It's a replica of the fountain in Copenhagen's Tivoli Park.

Gardens

Among the horticultural wonders on the 54-acre campus are a sunken rose garden and a lane of Japanese cherry trees that make for a glorious walk. And then there's the Moon Tree, a Douglas fir that rode on one of the Apollo missions as a seedling and now grows near Tivoli Fountain.

Capitol Lake

The lake cannot be used for swimming or boating but it's a popular spot with walkers, bicyclists and dog-walkers, who circle it. It was designed as a reflecting pool for the Capitol Dome and is on the northern extension of the campus. Access is from Heritage Park at Fifth Avenue and Water Street, from Marathon Park on the Deschutes Parkway or from the main campus via a gentle switchback trail.

State Capital Museum

Housed in the historic Lord Mansion, the Museum features exhibits on state history and Native culture. It's open Saturdays only but worth a visit even when closed to enjoy the lovely architecture and the native species garden that surrounds the building.
• 211 21st Ave. SW • 360.753.2580
• wshs.org/scmoc

South Capital Neighborhood

The entire neighborhood, which includes examples of pretty much every architectural style of the early 20th century, has been placed on the National Historic Register. The rough boundaries are Capitol Lake, 16th Avenue and I-5. A walking tour brochure is available at olympiawa. gov/city-services/historic-preservation/walking-tours-of-historic-olympia.aspx. This is, admittedly, a very long web address. Among the highlights, besides the State Capital Museum housed in the Lord Mansion, are the McCleary Mansion, 111 21st Ave. SW, Olympia, and the historic Mission Revival Lincoln Elementary School 213 21st Ave. SE

Best Area Book Stores *by Mark Lindquist*

King's Books

King's rules the South Sound. People come here for the diverse collection of used books, as well as readings, community events, a fat cat and a co-owner named sweet pea. If you live in Tacoma, you're almost certain to run into someone you know, so give yourself some extra time when you visit. • 218 St. Helens, Tacoma • 253.272.8801 • kingsbookstore.com

Tacoma Book Center

More than any other book store I know, TBC smells like a bookstore. I mean this in a good way. The non-descript window-less building looks like a warehouse for cocaine distribution, but inside it is books, books, books. You can get lost, literally. • 324 East 26th, Tacoma, • 253.572.8248 • tacomabookcenter.com

Culpepper Books

Culpepper specializes in rare and out-of-print books. I go here when I'm looking for a first edition. Located in the Proctor District near a Starbucks and good restaurants, it's relatively upscale. The owner is the brother of a local judge, so beware of lawyers lurking in the stacks. • 2521 N. Proctor, Tacoma • 253.761.9000 • culpepperbooks.com

Orca Books

Like many good indie book stores, Orca is a community hub with the requisite helpful staff, readings, and events. They have cool tee-shirts. • 509 4th Ave. E, Olympia • 360.352.0123 • orcabooks.com

Last Word Books

Advertising itself as "fiercely independent," Last Word has a far-lefty vibe even for an indie bookstore. Comfortable chairs are located throughout and nobody will hassle you for sitting there all day and reading 'zines, except maybe the evil store cat. 211 E 4th Ave., Olympia, 360.786.WORD, lastwordbooks.org

Whodunit Books

As you would expect from the name, mystery novels are the thing at Who-dunit. This is the South Sound's answer to Seattle's Mystery Bookstore. •301 4th Ave. W, Olympia •360.352.8252

Fireside Book Store

What's cool about Fireside is their emphasis on contemporary literature and their support of local authors. •Inside the Olympia Hotel at 116 Legion Way SE, Olympia •360.352.4006

A Good Book

If you buy books for children, as I now do, you will appreciate the upstairs children's section. As a further bonus, there's also a small cafe. •1014 Main, Sumner •253.891.9692 •indiebound.org

Revolving Books

Here the emphasis is on trading books. You enter with your "gently read" books, receive store credit, and exit with someone else's books. It's like recycling. •8021 Steilacoom Blvd. SW, Lakewood •253.584.6883 •revolvingbooks.qwestoffice.net

Mostly Books

Used books, new books, knowledgeable staff and - because this is Gig Harbor - nautical books and maps. Across the street from the Gig Harbor Marina, this is the only bookstore I know of with a water view from the front porch. •3126 Harborview Dr., Gig Harbor •253.851.3219 •mostlybooks.com

A Novel Idea

Opened in 2010. You have to admire anyone who would start a bookstore in these digital times and in this economy. Besides used books, they sell Peace of Earth pottery and other local arts. •116 South Meridian, Puyallup •253.840.BOOK •anovelideausedbooks.com

Mark Lindquist *is Pierce County Prosecutor. His novels include The King of Methlehem, published by Simon & Schuster in 2007, and Never Mind Nirvana, published by Random House in 2001. He has reviewed books for The New York Times Book Review, The Los Angeles Times, The Oregonian, and the Seattle Times.*

East Olympia

Olympia's East Side is tucked between the funky downtown and Lacey's expansive growth, with parks, a marina and charming neighborhoods. To borrow a slogan from Maryland, the East Side is "Tree-mendous."

Molly Gilmore

Legion Way

The oak and sweetgum trees lining the street are a memorial to those who died in World War I. After almost a century the street remains a peaceful, shady place to walk.
• eastside-olympia.org

Neighborhood Tour

Beyond Legion Way, the city's walking tour for the Eastside includes historic homes and civic buildings as well as landmark trees.
• olympiawa.gov

Priest Point Park

Yes, trees. But much more. The 314 acres offers a mile of saltwater shoreline and views of downtown and the Capitol along the Ellis Cove Trail. • 2600 East Bay Dr. NE
• 360.753.8380 ❶

Bigelow House Museum

Built in the 1850s, the Carpenter Gothic-style Bigelow House is the oldest residence still standing in Olympia and one of the oldest in the Northwest.
• 918 Glass Ave. NE • 360.753.1215
• bigelowhouse.org ❷

Boston Harbor Marina

Boat, rentals, kayak tours, seafood in season; picnic with views of the Olympic Mountains and the South Sound.
• 312 73rd Ave. NE • 360.357.5670
• bostonharbormarina.com ❸

San Francisco Street Bakery

The bakery has everything from Danish and bagels to cookies and pies, plus sandwiches, good coffee and patio dining landscaped with native plants.
• 1320 San Francisco Ave. NE
• 360.753.8553 • sfsbakery.com ❹

Eastside Big Tom Drive Inn

This Olympia institution serves beef and veggie burgers (the owner is a vegetarian when not on the job) slathered with a secret sauce known as Goop • 2023 4th Ave. E
• 360.357.4852
• eastsidebigtom.com ❺

Olympia Little Theater

Olympia's oldest live theater offers bargain-priced amateur productions from the tried- and- true to offbeat. The season runs September to June. • 1925 Miller Ave. NE
• 360.786.9484
• olympialittletheater.org ❻

Eastside Co-op

Worth a visit for people-watching and the soup and salad bar. A small seating area. • 311 Pacific Ave. SE
• 360.956.3870
• olympiafood.coop ❼

Swantown Inn

A bed and breakfast in a Victorian mansion, with a very modern day spa. • 1431 11th Ave. SE
• 877.753.9123
• swantowninn.com ❽

Beauty Temple

Devoted to all-natural, environmentally-friendly beauty; services include facials, body wraps and pedicures in addition to hair care, in a lovely wooded setting. By appointment. • 726 Libby Rd. NE • 360.357.0275 ❾

Gravity Beer Market

Beer and beer only, with monthly tastings, beers on tap and over 600 beers to go.
• 1001 4th Ave. E • 360.352.5107
• gravitybeermarket.com ❿

Grand Vin Wine Merchants

If you prefer the grape to the grain, this wine shop is right next door. An emphasis on grand cru Bordeaux.
• 1003 4th Ave. E.
• 360.350.4896
• grandvinwinemerchants.com ⓫

Twister Donuts

Well beyond the traditional including a bacon-maple bar and ham-and-cheese filled doughnut. Tables, free wi-fi.
• 2302 Martin Way
• 360.489.0971 ⓬

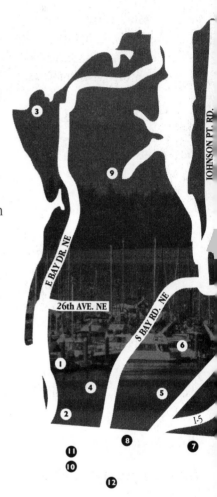

West Olympia

Just across Budd Inlet from downtown, Olympia's West Side is home to the mall and big boxes, but it's also filled with restful parks, distinctive meals and Evergreen – something of a park in itself.

Molly Gilmore

The Evergreen State College
It would be hard to overstate Evergreen's impact on Olympia and the state. The school's intellectual output flows through public policy, and the city's culture has been shaped by the tastes of students, faculty and alums. The campus includes more than 1,000 acres of forest and beaches, with a Japanese garden and organic farm thrown in for good measure. Interior spaces include the House of Welcome, a Longhouse built in collaboration with Northwest tribes; library and gallery; and food service in the student union. •2700 Evergreen Pkwy. NW •360.867.6000
•www.evergreen.edu ❶

McLane Creek Trail

Popular with runners and school-children alike, this boardwalk trail allows people of all ages and physical abilities to immerse themselves in the natural beauty of a wetland ecosystem. The Black Hills Audubon Society has named the trail one of South Sound's best places for birding. • Off Delphi Rd. • wta.org/go-hiking/hikes ❷

Grass Lake Nature Park

This 171-acre wetland refuge is home to more than 100 species of birds and more than 200 species of plants. • 814 Kaiser Rd. NW • 360.753.8380 • olympiawa.gov ❸

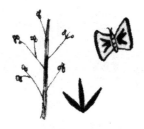

Yauger Park

Amidst the diversity of parks on the West Side this one is for sports, with three ball fields and an 11,500-square-foot skate court. • 3100 Capital Mall Dr. SW • 360.753.8380 • olympiawa.gov ❹

Garfield Nature Trail

This trail takes suburban explorers from West Bay Drive to Rogers Street, where they can find sustenance or explore the neighborhood. • 620 Rogers St. NW • 360.753.8380 • olympiawa.gov ❺

Sage's Brunch House

Sage's serves one of Olympia's best breakfasts, but be prepared to take your time. (Brunch is, after all, a leisurely meal.) There's sweet outside seating, too. • 903 Rogers St. NW • 360.352.1103 • sagesbrunchhouse.com ❻

Westside Co-op

This neighborhood institution is a good source of organic take-out. 8 a.m. to 9 p.m. seven days. • 921 Rogers St. NW • 360.754.7666 • olympiafood.coop ❼

Kenneth J. Minnaert Center for the Arts

Located on the campus of South Puget Sound Community College, the Center hosts professional, college and community performances, films and more. Gallery. • 2011 Mottman Rd. SW • 360.754.7711 • washingtoncenter.org ❽

Vic's Pizzeria

Creative combinations, vegan options and fresh sparkling limeade. • 233 Division St. NW • 360.943.8044 • eatatvics.net ❾

Mandelin's

Recycling and reusing is the Olympia way. So is having your own distinctive style. This well-stocked consignment shop meets both needs. • 222 Division St. NW • 360.628.8718 • mandelins.com ❿

Blue Heron Bakery

If Olympia is the classic crunchy-granola kind of place, the granola probably comes from this wholesome bakery.

- 4935 Mud Bay Rd. NW
- 360.866.2253
- blueheronbakery.com ⓫

Olympia Coffee Roasting Co.

A favorite of Westsiders, who rave about this tiny spot's espresso — and its garden seating.

- 1706 Harrison Ave. NW
- 360.705.9451
- olympiacoffee.com ⓬

Mud Bay Coffee Co.

This shop also has locally roasted coffee, plus ample seating, a drive-through window and a performance stage including improv.

- 1600 Cooper Point Rd. SW
- 360.754.6222
- mudbaycoffee.com ⓭

The Eld House

B&B cottage on the shore of the southern-most inlet on Puget Sound. Kayaks.

- 5531 Sunrise Beach Rd. NW
- 360.866.2356 or daytime at 360.701.8388 ⓮

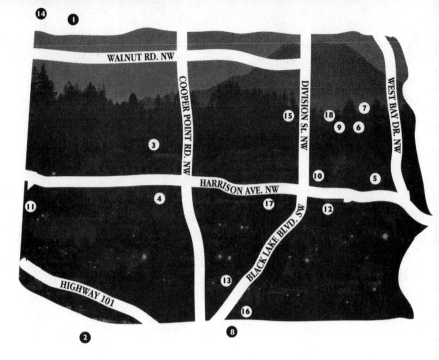

Off Leash Dog Area
505 Bing NW ⓯

Shankz Black Light Miniature Golf
This is a little hard to explain; involves 3-D glasses, jungle animals and dinosaurs. Plus putters. Located next to IHOP, making life a bit more contrapuntal. • 1520 SW Cooper Pt. Rd. • 360.943.1715
• shankzglowgolf.com ⓰

Iron Rabbit
Few rabbit holes in the wall serve prawns, cod and smoked salmon in a creamy dill sauce under mashed potatoes and topped with cheese. Chef can respond to many dietary needs. Fine food, craft beers, artful space. • 2103 Harrison NW
• 360.956.3661
• ironrabbit.net ⓱

Chez Cascadia
Olympia's only hostel, privately owned and operated in a charming house. A dorm room sleeps nine in bunk beds; a private room – for that semi-hostel experience – has a double bed. Bathroom, laundry, towels and bedding. Vegetarian kitchen available for guest use.
• 323 Milroy NW • 360.570.0823
• chezcascadia.org ⓲

Port of Olympia

Shops, art, dining, plus museums and more on and near the water at the foot of Puget Sound. A beautiful place for an evening stroll.

Alec Clayton

Farmers Market
Homegrown fruits and vegetables, meats, clothing, arts and crafts sold by local vendors. Open April through October Thursday through Sunday, and Saturday and Sunday in November and December.
- 700 Capitol Way N
- 360.352.9096
- olympiafarmersmarket.com ❶

Percival Landing
The recently rebuilt boardwalk at Percival Landing is great for strolling with fabulous scenes overlooking Budd Inlet East Bay. There are restaurants, a gallery, gift shops, a huge plaza and a viewing tower.
- 217 Thurston Ave. NW, parking is available at 405 Columbia St. NW
- olympiawa.gov ❷

Public Art at Percival Landing

Public art scattered throughout the boardwalk area includes Tide Pool of Time by Brian Goldbloom and David Vala, a pool with seafarer memorabilia, Motherhood, an 11-foot tall statue of a pregnant woman by Simon Kogen and Triumph of the Vegetables by Jean Whitesavage; Nick Lyle created the forged steel latticework at the roundabout in front of the Olympia Farmers Market. The landing extends from 4th Avenue to the Farmers Market.

Budd Bay Cafe

With a view of the bay snow-capped Olympics and to the capitol dome, Budd Bay offers seafood in a comfortable, homey environment — mostly booth seating with tables along the water-facing windows and a large patio for outdoor dining when the weather is suitable. Open for breakfast at 6:30 a.m. Monday through Saturday and for Sunday brunch staring at 9:30 a.m.
• 525 Columbia St. NW
• 360.357.6963
• buddbaycafe.com ➌

Dancing Goats Espresso Bar

Worn out from wandering the market and the waterfront? Take a break across the street at Dancing Goats. It's an Italian style espresso bar that features coffee from Batdorf & Bronson Roaster. Batdorf is to Olympia what Starbucks is to Seattle. • 111 Market St. NE ➍
• 360.528.8555 • dancinggoats.com

Batdorf and Bronson Tasting Room

Competing with their own espresso bar directly across the street, the Batdorf tasting room and roastery offers a variety of coffees to sample from the major growing areas of Africa, Indonesia and Latin America. Limited hours and limited seating.
• 200 Market St. NE • 360.753.4057
• batdorfcoffee.com ➎

Olympia Weekend Market

Geisha dolls, doll houses, microphone stands, clothing, turntables and lots of antiques at this market. Open Saturday and Sunday 10 a.m. to 5 p.m. year-round with vendors selling antiques, art, records, jewelry, tools and more. New vendors and items every weekend. • 210 Thurston Ave. NE • 360.464.0048
• olymarket.weebly.com ➏

WET Science Center

WET stands for Water Education and Technology, and the science center is an educational museum of the LOTT Clean Water Alliance's education program. It's new, state of the art and hands-on. WET Science Center provides fun ways to learn all about water, where it comes from, where it goes and how to save and recycle it.
• Thurston Ave. at Adams St.
• 360.664.2333
• lottcleanwater.org ➐

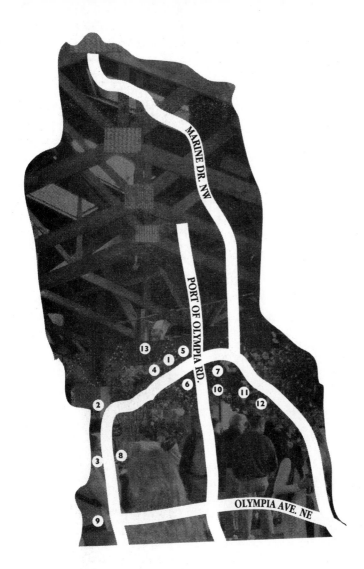

The Wine Loft

It's a big wine store in a tiny historic building on the waterfront, offering tastings indoors and out. • 401 Columbia St. NW • 360.754.6208 • wineloftoly.com ❽

The Olympia Seafood Company

This is another big surprise in a nondescript little building at Percival Landing, offering a selection of local and exotic fresh fish and shellfish, including fresh shucked oysters, as well as hot clam chowder and seafood cocktails to go.
• 411 Columbia St. NW
• 360.570.8816
• olympiaseafood.com ❾

Warehouse Rock Gym

From the outside it's a featureless warehouse. Inside an art installation of varied and multicolored climbing walls with climbing and classes for all levels of expertise.
• 315 Jefferson St. NE
• 360.596.9255
• warehouserockgym.com ❿

Alpine Experience

This local, family-owned outdoor retailer has everything for the hiker, backpacker, skier and camper including clothing and equipment sales, repair and rentals.
• 408 Olympia Ave. • 360.956.1699
• alpinex.com ⓫

Oly Geek

People who don't know what to do with their old computers can take them to Oly Geek to be recycled or sold for a small fee. This all-volunteer organization gives free working computers to non-profits. They also have very inexpensive computers and parts for sale.
• 115 Olympia Ave.
• oly-wa.us/OlyGeek ⓬

Gardner's Seafood and Pasta

Traditional menu in an intimate setting. Lots of local wines, full bar.
• 111 Thurston Way NW
• 360.786.8466
• gardnersrestaurant.com ⓭

Yelm

The Coast Salish word shelm (or chelm) speaks to the mirage of heat emanating from the prairie; Yelm in summer is hot. Wet perhaps, but hot. The area was home to the Nisqually tribe, whose horses thrived on the vast pasture lands. Later, proximity to the Northern Pacific terminus in Tacoma meant Yelm's farm and forest products had ready access to market. Today Yelm is one of the state's fastest growing cities, convenient to Olympia, JBLM and Tacoma.

Jesse Michener

Flanagans Apple Irish Pub
Open mic each week, good pub food and a great vibe.
704 W Yelm Ave. 360.400.2300
flanagansapple.org ❶

Fadi's
Located at the Tahoma Valley Golf and Country Club. Serving breakfast, lunch and dinner at reasonable prices.

• 15425 Mosman Ave. SW ❷
• 360.400.3500 fadisrestaurant.com

The Spiral Cafe
All-natural rotisserie chicken and a mean gyro. Good coffee, yoga classes, a stage for music. It's the basic cool-kids hang out. • 201 E Yelm Ave. • 360.400.2233
• spiralcafe.net ❸

Yelm Food Co-Op and Farmers Market

As of April, 2012 Yelm Food Co-Op and Gordon's Garden Center share space – and a mission: sourcing organic and sustainable food. The Market, launched in May, is looking for a permanent location.
• 308 E Yelm Ave. • 360.400.2210
• yelmfood.coop.com ❹

JZ Rose

An eclectic blend of antiques, reclaimed goods and the sometimes unusual.
• 207 1st St. S • 360.458.4618
• jz-rose.com ❺

Yelm-Tenino Trail

Almost 15 miles of the larger Western Chehalis Trail. Runs along de-commissioned railroad track through remarkably diverse landscapes, including wetlands, prairie, farms, forests and creeks.
• 105 Yelm Ave. W (trailhead starts behind City Hall)
• co.thurston.wa.us ❻

The Prairie Hotel

This is a well-appointed medium-sized hotel with reasonable prices. Convenient to most everything in downtown Yelm. • 700 Prairie Park Ln. • 360.458.8300
• prairiehotel.com ❼

Yelm City Park

Hosts city-wide events each year, including Prairie Days, Octoberfest, Christmas in the Park, Yelm Lions Easter Egg Hunt and a summer car show. Skate park, covered pavilion, playground and general merriment, the kind of small-town park that brings everyone together.
• SR 507 & Mosman Ave. ❽

Cochrane Park

Eight acres, four of which are wetlands involved in water reclamation. The reclaimed water is used all over the city including the Cochrane Park pond, where families can enjoy catch and release fishing.
• ci.yelm.wa.us ❾

Gordon's Garden Center

Gordon's boasts the largest selection of roses around and a knowledgeable staff.
• 308 E Yelm Ave. • 360.458.2481
• gordonsgardencenter.com ❿

Prairie Lanes

The staff is friendly and won't blink if patrons want to bowl with the bumpers up.
202 E Yelm Ave.
• yelmprairielanes.com ⓫

Tahoma Valley Golf

Affordable greens fees and a well-maintained course.
• 15425 Mosman Ave. SW
• 360.458-3332 ⓬

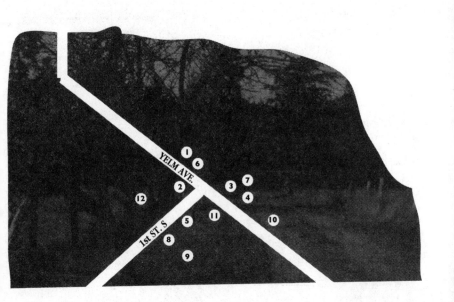

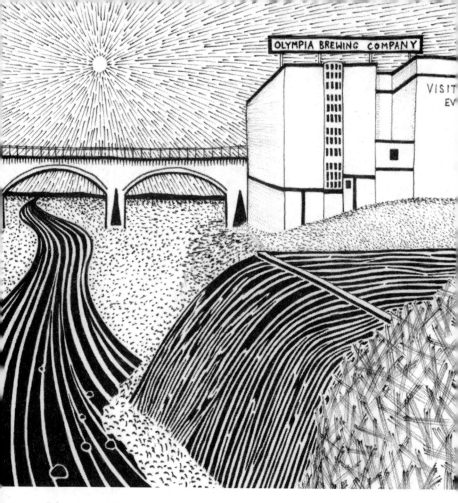

The text in the image reads: "OLYMPIA BREWING COMPANY" and "VISIT EV"

Tumwater

Proudly proclaiming itself Washington's oldest city, Tumwater is home to many parks and government offices, the old Olympia Brewery and the old brewhouse on the Deschutes River, both regrettably closed and crumbling.

Alec Clayton

Tumwater Hill Park

The half mile looped nature trail at Tumwater Hill Park whisks quickly away from the nearby housing developments to nothing but trees. Steep slopes including stairs at the start. The trailhead entrance is at Tumwater Hill Elementary School
• 3120 Ridgeview Ct. SW ❶

Falls Terrace Restaurant

Known for its spectacular views, seating at Falls Terrace overlooks the Tumwater Falls Park. The lunch menu includes such tasty treats as filet of salmon baked in white wine and butter or poached with fresh dill and crab au gratin topped with hollandaise and cheddar.
• 106 Deschutes Way SW
• 360.943.7830 • fallsterrace.com ❷

158

Mason Jar

It's been called cute as kittens, which was meant as a compliment. Definitely a homey kind of restaurant with an early-American kitchen feel. Open limited hours for breakfast and lunch, 9 a.m. to 4 p.m. weekdays. • 408 Cleveland Ave. SE • 360.754.7776 • themasonjar.net ❸

South Sound Running

These folks are serious about running. It's the place to go for information on races, for training and equipment. (Also in Tacoma's University District.) • 3405 Capitol Blvd. SW • 360.705.2580 • southsoundrunning.com ❹

Just Keep Swimming

Indoor pools are open year-round but department stores sell swimwear only seasonally. Problem solved with Just Keep Swimming, open year-round with competitive and recreational swimming gear for all ages. • 3413 Capitol Way Blvd. SW • 360.705.0384 • justkeepswimminginc.com ❺

Uncork & Unwind

Located in a distinctive black house with tan trim, this wine bar specializes in Washington state wines with an emphasis on small wineries. Fifty bottles open for flights or servings by the glass. • 324 Custer Way SW • 360.943.WINE • uncorkandunwind.net ❻

Western Meats

This is where Olympia area meat lovers go to get ready for a big cookout. They sell all kinds of meat; the sausage are housemade at the Blue Max sausage kitchen in Puyallup. • 4101 Capitol Blvd. SW • 360.357.6601 • westernmeats.net ❼

El Sarape

El Sarape has been serving traditional Mexican meals for 30 years. Private party reservations are available. And there's a cozy bar. (Also in Olympia and Lacey.) • 5409 Capitol Blvd. SW • 360.956.9506 • elsarape.net ❽

Sri's Corner

Sri's Corner serves South Indian cuisine in a bright and roomy environment; reasonably priced buffet lunches and sit-down dinners. The masala dosa and butter chicken are recommended. • 5109 Capitol Blvd. SE Suite E • 360.539.2027 • sriscorner.com ❾

Eagan's Drive-In

It's a tiny drive-in fast food burger joint with a 1950s diner feel. Burgers and espresso. • 6400 Capitol Blvd. SE • 360.357.9349 ❿

Tumwater Falls Park

The half-mile walking trail skirts both banks of the Deschutes River, past raging waterfalls in the shadow of the closed-down Olympia Brewery with a view of the brewhouse. There is a spacious park area with picnic facilities, restrooms and children's playground.
• 110 Deschutes Parkway ⓫

The Old Brewhouse

Listed as one of Washington's 10 most endangered historic properties by the Washington Trust for Historic Preservation, the Old Brewhouse is six stories tall of red brick and in serious disrepair. It is best viewed from Tumwater Falls Park. • 110 Deschutes Parkway ⓬

Henderson House Museum

This small but attractive Victorian home built in 1905 features attractive bay windows and a second story turret. It has been closed to tours (indefinitely) since October 2011 but is fun to view from the outside. • 602 Deschutes Way
• 360.754.4217 ⓭

Crosby House Museum

One of the oldest wood-frame houses in the state, the Crosby House was built in 1860. The adjacent rose garden boasts rose varieties from the 1860s. Tours are offered Fridays and Saturdays, March to November. Next door to the Henderson House. • 602 Deschutes Way • 360.943.9884 ⓮

Tumwater Historical Park

It's a small park with a large covered picnic area and children's play area, a short hiking trail and the closest views anywhere of the abandoned historic Brewhouse. The entrance is adjacent to the Henderson and Crosby houses. ⓯

The Brick on Trosper

The Brick is a large family restaurant with an equally large menu featuring wood fired pizza cooked in a brick oven, steaks, salmon, halibut, and a large selection of appetizers. The "baseball cut," is round and thick and carved by hand.
• 707 Trosper Rd. SW
• 360.753.6626
• thebrickontrosper.com ⓰

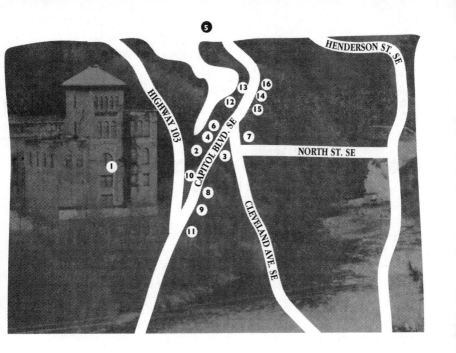

Lacey

Sprawling from Olympia to the Nisqually Delta just south of Joint Base Lewis McChord, Lacey has no downtown but miles of shopping centers and big box stores and parks.

Alec Clayton

Boomerang Music and Video

Specializing in used CDs and DVDs restored to like-new condition; also posters, incense, Olympia Beer memorabilia and hard to find items.
• 700 Sleater Kinney Rd. SE in Market Square (between Fred Meyer and Starbucks) • 360.413.9118
• boomerangmusicvideo.com ❶

Curry Corner

This tiny Indian restaurant consistently has rave reviews.
• 9408 Martin Way E • 360.455.8776
• currycorner.us ❷

Copper Creek Coffee

Some folks claim this little coffee hut has the best mochas in town. Their coffee is roasted by Dillanos in Sumner, voted Coffee Roaster of the Year by Roast Magazine. Limited food menu.
• 4120 Martin Way E. • 360.923.1300
• coppercreekcafe.com ❸

Tofu Hut

Despite the name, it's not just tofu. The Tofu Hut caters to meat eaters as well as vegetarians and vegans. Vegan and gluten-free desserts and wheat-free soy sauce available, and brown rice is always an option.
• 4804 Pacific Ave. SE
• 360.456.8638
• tofuhutrestaurant.com ❹

Classic Winemakers

This micro winery specializes in small batches. Very small. Blending available. Wine tastings, wine by the bottle and wine making supplies.
• 1225 Ruddell Rd. SE
• 360.493.6500
• classicwinemakers.com ❺

Chehalis Western Trail

The biking and hiking trail has four sets of trailhead facilities in Lacey with parking, restrooms, and picnic; Chambers Lake boat launch; scenic overlook at Chambers Lake; the Yelm Highway pedestrian overpass; and 67th Avenue, with a parking area at Fir Tree Road. **❻**

Chambers Lake

The park is currently undeveloped; the lake has a boat launch. There is also a trail head to the Chehalis Western Trail. •3725 14th Ave.

Monks Cemetery at St. Martin's University

It's walled and gated, and has headstones of Benedictine monks from way back. Neat old names. Especially fun on a dark and stormy night. •5000 Abbey Way SE **❼**

Long Lake

This lake near the Thurston County Fairgrounds offers one of the few swimming beaches in Thurston County, with sandy shoreline, barbeque and picnic facilities and walking trails through the woods.
• 2790 Carpenter Rd. **❽**

Shipwreck Beads

It may be hard to believe the world's largest bead seller is located in a big industrial warehouse in Lacey. But here it is, aisle after aisle of cargo-loads of sparkly beads. Shop in person or online or from the gigantic catalog.
• 8560 Commerce Pl. Dr. NE
• 360.754.2323
• shipwreckbeads.com **❾**

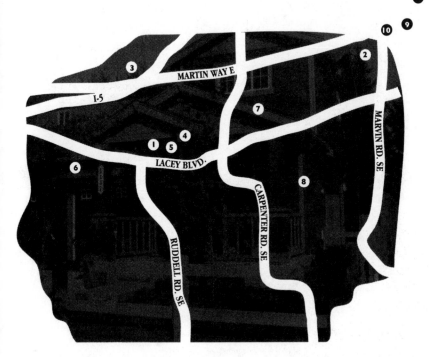

Marvin Road Golf and Batting Range

This place has it all, from miniature golf with water hazards to a batting range with heated cages to a 32-foot tall rock climbing tower. Well, that's a lot if not all. • 2831 Marvin Rd. NE • marvinroadminigolf.com ❿

Nisqually Reach Nature Center

A chance to get muddy and learn about nature at this environmental education center by the Luhr Beach boat launch and fishing access. • D'Milluhr Dr. NE • 360.459.0387 • nisquallyestuary.org ⓫

Nisqually Delta

The Nisqually Delta is a temperate coastal salt marsh and a major resting area for migratory waterfowl in the southern Puget Sound region. In 1974, Nisqually National Wildlife Refuge was established to protect the delta and its diversity of fish and wildlife habitats. The Nisqually estuary was restored in 2009 by removing dikes and reconnecting 762 acres with the tides of Puget Sound. This is the largest estuary restoration project in the Pacific Northwest and an important step in the recovery of Puget Sound.

L. Lisa Lawrence

Nisqually Wildlife Refuge

Situated on the Nisqually Delta, this 3,000 acre wildlife refuge encompasses both salt water and freshwater habitat. It features a newly completed boardwalk, an interpretive center, trails and educational opportunities. In cooperation with the Nisqually Tribe, the area is being reclaimed and returned to its natural state, to promote salmon and other wildlife.
- 100 Brown Farm Rd.
- 360.753-9467
- fws.gov/Nisqually ❶

165

Luhr's Landing Boat Launch

It's possible to explore the Nisqually Reach and delta by boat, by putting in at this public launch. Open year round; restrooms.
- 4949 D'Milluhr Dr. NE
- 360.249.4628 ❷

The Inn At Mallard Cove

Located on the shores of Puget Sound near the mouth of the Nisqually Delta. This elegant bed and breakfast provides a peaceful respite, with views of the Olympic Mountains.
- 5025 Meridian Rd. NE
- 360.491.9795
- theinnatmallardcove.com ❸

Sweet Tease Kitty B & B

A place where Fluffy will be treated like royalty while the humans are off on adventure. A B&B just for kitties.
- 505 Torden Ln. SE • 360.464.7663
- sweetteazekittybb.com ❹

Medicine Creek Winery

A boutique winery specializing in reds. The historic building is said to resemble an 1800's bordello; this may be a plus.
- 947 Old Pacific Hwy. SE
- 360.701.6284
- medicinecreekwinery.com ❺

Madsen Family Cellars

All the grapes used by this friendly, family winery are sourced from Eastern Washington. The tasting room offers almost two dozen wines.
- 2825 Marvin Rd. NE suite D
- 360.438.1286
- madsenfamilycellars.com ❻

Nisqually Red Wind Casino

In addition to the usual amenities, gaming, entertainment and dining found in regional casinos, this one boasts a remarkable seafood buffet.
- 12819 Yelm Hwy • 360.412.5000
- redwindcasino.com ❼

Nisqually Bar and Grill

A favorite local hangout, the Nisqually Bar and Grill is family friendly and noted for chicken fried steak and home style burgers. ❽
- 10323 Martin Way E • 360.491.6123

Nisqually Plaza RV Park

This park provides easy access to I-5 in a wooded park-like setting. Short- and long-term sites. ❾
- 10220 Martin Way E • 360.491.3831

Woodlands Golf Course

One of two courses, the Woodland Course is scenic and friendly. The Links course at Hawks Prairie is a tougher challenge.
- 4550 Meriwood Dr. NE
- 360.412.0459
- hawksprairiegolf.com **10**

William B Ives Trail

A 1.5 mile wooded trail from the Meridian Neighborhood Park, through a nature preserve with lovely views of the Woodlands Golf Course. Trailhead at Meridian Neighborhood Park
- 8855 Campus Glen Dr. NE
- 360.491.3214 • ci.lacey.wa.us

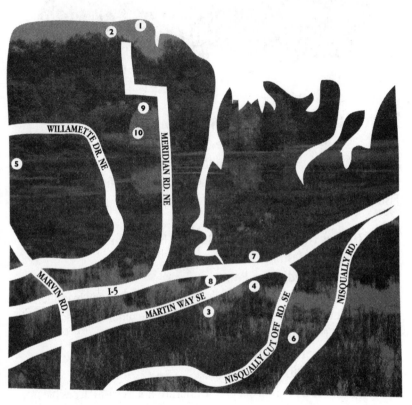

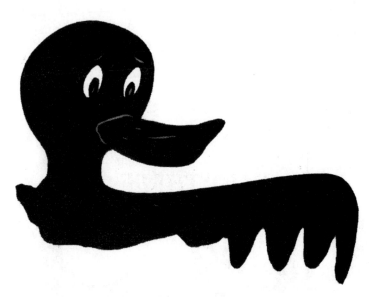

Favorite Birding Sites *by Helen Engle*

Because Washington has so many different eco-systems, we have a wide diversity of birds, both resident and migrant. I've done field work for US Fish &Wildlife Refuges for a long time and my favorites places are:

Grays Harbor National Wildlife Refuge (Bowerman Basin in spring!)
Protection Island (from tour boats)
Willapa Bay & Leadbetter Point
The San Juan Islands (with the added attraction of marine mammals)
Commencement Bay (huge flocks of Grebes are diminishing so fast)
Chambers Creek Estuary
Puyallup Valley Farmland
Titlow Park (for birds in the Narrows)
Fort Lewis (The oak-savannah prairie area are not as easily accesible now with Homeland Security)
My Own Garden (all year round)

Helen Engle is a co-founder of Tahoma Audubon and a 20-year member of the National Audubon board. Birding maps for the entire state are available at wa.audubon.org/great-washington-state-birding-trail

▲▲▲

PART THREE:
MASON COUNTY

Mason County

More than many places, Mason County is defined by its natural setting. The northwest quadrant of the county is national forest; Hood Canal – a slender finger of Puget Sound – runs through the northeast. The map is dotted with lakes and lined by twisting roads; the Olympics loom over the Pacific, hiding rain forest within and rocky shore below. This is long-drive country, rugged, with small, scattered settlements, great beauty and some special places to eat and stay, indoors and out. It's like nowhere else on earth.

L. Lisa Lawrence and Courtenay Chamberlain

Olympic National Forest and Park

The Forest
Surrounds the Park and has several distinct wilderness areas. It also boasts one of the few national forest campgrounds located on salt water with oysters for public harvest.
• 360.956.2402
• fs.usda.gov/Olympic

Lake Quinault and Rainforest
This micro-climate receives 144 inches of rain annually, so the forest is steamy, with lush vines and ferns thriving in the shadow of giant conifers. Wildlife is abundant. The sparkling blue lake is great for boating, swimming and fishing.
• fs.usda.gov/recarea/Olympic

Lake Quinault Lodge
Nestled in the Rain Forest and set on the lakeshore, this historic grand lodge offers rooms in the main building [some with fireplaces], in the newer lakeside building and in the renovated boathouse. Dining room and gift shop. The large fireplace in the great room encourages curling up with a good e-reader.
• 345 South Shore Rd.
• 800.562.6672
• olympicnationalparks.com

Seal Rock Campground
Seal Rock has two distinctions: it's one of the few National Forest campgrounds on salt water; and the public can harvest oysters. • On Hood Canal, 2 miles north of Brinnon on U.S. Highway 101

Hood Canal Ranger District Trails
There are numerous scenic trails here including the Big Creek Loop, Buckhorn Lake Trail, Lena Lake Trail, Mt Townsend and Big and Little Quilcene Trails. Maps for these trails - including the Dungeness area trails out of Sequim – on line. • 360.765.2200
• fs.usda.gov/recarea/Olympic

The Park
Waves crashing on the ocean shore, temperate rain forest, flower filled meadows and mountain peaks … all part of nearly a million acres; 95 percent have been declared wilderness and wild they are. U.S. Highway 101 reaches all parts of the Park. • 360.565.3130
• nps.gov/olym

Kalaloch Lodge and Coastal Beaches
The Kalaloch area has a stunning series of beaches, including the jewel, Ruby Beach. The historic lodge provides spectacular views and easy access to the beaches and two rain forests.
• Exit off of U.S. 101 • 360.962.2271
• olympicnationalparks.com

Sol Duc Hot Springs Resort

The Resort has accommodations for varied tastes including cabins and suites. The main attraction is of course the hot mineral pools. Other amenities include spa, restaurant, cafe, convenience store and gift shop. • 12076 Sol Duc Hot Springs Rd., Port Angeles • 360.327.3583 • olympicnationalpark.com

Lake Crescent

Lake Crescent has boating and fishing and many opportunities for hiking, as well as for mountain biking on the Iron Horse Trail.

The Lake Crescent Lodge and Log Cabin Resort

Both provide various lodging and dining options. 87 lakeside camp sites, a swimming beach and general store in walking distance. • nps.gov/olym

Hoh Rain Forest

The Hoh Rainforest Visitor Center is located at the end of Upper Hoh Road and offers a campground and nature trails. • Access off Hoh Rd. from Highway 101 about an hour north of Forks • 360.374.6925 • nps.gov/olym

Olympic Hot Springs

Earthy sulfurous pools, for a more rustic hot springs experience. Due to the Elwah River restoration project the Olympic Hot Springs Road is closed through summer of 2013. The only access during this time is a 14-mile hike from the Sol Duc Valley via Appleton Pass. The advantage? Not much of a crowd. • Olympic Hot Springs Rd., Port Angeles • 360.565.3130 • olympic.national-park.com

Lake Ozette

Includes a Park Service campground, boat launch and boardwalk trails through old growth forest to the beach. • nps.gov/olym

Lost Resort at Lake Ozette

Campsites, cabins, showers, a general store and deli. • 208660 Hoko-Ozette Rd., Clallam Bay • 800.950.2899 • lostresort.net

Elwah River

Though north of the Park and Forest – and of Mason County for that matter - it's well worth watching this project: the historic decommissioning and removal of the Elwha and Glines Canyon dams; and restoration of the Elwha to a free flowing river, with 70 miles of pristine passage to spawning grounds and habitat for native salmon and other wildlife. This is the largest dam removal project in U.S. history, scheduled to continue through 2013. • The project can be reached on the Olympic Hot Springs Road off Hwy 101 about 10 miles south of Port Angeles. • Gov/olym/nature-scienceelwha-ecosystem-restoration

Belfair

Situated on the Union River and a convenient gateway to Hood Canal and the Olympic Peninsula's rich mix of recreation and relaxation. In addition to the amenities listed here, Belfair offers a number of stores for camping, hiking, and picnic provisions.

Theler Community Center and Wetland

Birdwatchers, photographers, runners and walkers dot the four miles of barrier-free woods and wetland trails and boardwalks. Open daily, free. Exhibit center open weekends and holidays. No pets.

- 22871 NE State Route 3
- 360.275.4898
- thelercenter.org

Belfair Farmer's Market

Before a wetland trail walk, perhaps a wooden toy, local produce or something hand-sewn. Saturdays May-September.

- 22871 NE State Route 3
- belfairfarmersmarket.org

The Farm at Water's Edge

The Hood Canal Salmon Enhancement Group's chemical-free garden, with alpaca, llama, Nubian goats and cage-free chickens. Fresh eggs by donation. The Farm is accessible by car or from the Theler trails.
- 600 NE Roessel Rd.
- 360.275.3575

Scott McLendon's Hardware

For anything forgotten. Plus it's fun to cruise the overstuffed aisles of home, garden and recreation gear.
- 51 State Route 300 • 360.275.0113
- scottmclendonshardware.com

North Mason Branch Timberland Regional Library

Nestled among large Douglas firs, this is a pleasant destination on wet days [see rain forest, above] or when the tide is too low for swimming. Public computers and free wi-fi, children's story hours.
- 23081 NE State Route 3
- 360.275.3232 trlib.org

Seabeck Pizza

This local chain offers pizza lots of ways: thin crust, thick crust, take-and-bake, to go, dine in, whole pie, or a slice. Subs and salads, too.
- NE 11 Old Belfair • 360.275.2657
- seabeckpizza.com

Casper's Pizza and BBQ

Pizzas and pulled pork are favorites, accompanied by a good draft beer, of course. Kid friendly, pleasant staff, mascot bulldog, also pleasant; it's just not so obvious.
- 23730 NE State Route 3
- 360.275.7427

Belfair State Park

Kayak launch and shellfish harvesting. Year-round camping. Kids enjoy the creeks for dam building fun and fall salmon runs. Day-use Discover Pass required.
- 3151 NE State Route 300
- 888.CAMPOUT
- parks.wa.gov/parks

Hood Canal

This natural waterway separates the Kitsap and Olympic Peninsulas. Captain George Vancouver explored the area in 1792, naming it after Royal Navy Admiral Lord Samuel Hood; a shrewd career move. One of the warmest saltwater bodies in Puget Sound, the Canal is ideal for swimming, boating, fishing, and shellfish harvesting.
- Check regulations and closures at wdfw.wa.gov

Hoodsport Winery
One of the state's earliest wineries [founded 1978], Hoodsport features merlots, syrahs and cabs as well as fruit wines. Also locally roasted coffee, jam and chocolate wine truffles. Canal view from the tasting room. • 23501 Hwy. 101 • 360.877.9894
• hoodsport.com

Lake Cushman Resort
With 4,000 acres and 23 miles of shoreline, the Resort offers peaceful wandering and water sports including sailing, scuba diving, water skiing and swimming. Privately owned, casual, family friendly, with tent and RV camping sites as well as rustic cabins; convenience store and boat rentals. • 4621 N Lake Cushman Rd. • 360.877.9630
• lakecushman.com

Allyn
Bookended by two public parks with water access. On the north, Waterfront Park offers a playground, boat launch, dock, and gazebo. It hosts town celebrations, weddings, concerts, and picnics. South is Kayak Park, perfect for picnics and beach combing.

Bear in a Box - George Kenny School of Chainsaw Carving
An impressive collection of chainsaw bears and sculptures, carvers at work and chainsaw-carving lessons.
• 8351 E State Route 3
• 360.275.9570 • bearinabox.com

Allyn Knit and Spinning Shop
A very nice collection of yarns; spinning wheels and supplies.
• 18462 Highway 3 • 360.275.4729
• allynknitandspin.com

Lennard K's
We've all been to a place like this: good burgers, great view, a sort of Jimmy Buffet head set. Kids welcome in dining room. • 18340 State Route 3 • 360.275.6060
• lennardks.com

Grapeview
This small waterfront community was home to the Pacific Northwest's first vineyards and winery. Fair Harbor Marina has a general store and guest moorage.
• Moorage: 5050 E Grapeview Loop Rd. • 360.426.4028
• fairharbormarina.com

Jarrel Cove and nearby campgrounds
Forested park on Harstine Island's northwest end is accessible by road and boat; campsites near docks and in rolling meadow. Jarrel Cove administers five additional parks: Harstine, McMicken, Stretch, Eagle and Hope Island. Harstine is for day use. Others are accessible only by boat; buoy moorage available. Day-use Discover Pass required.
• 391 E Wingert Rd. Shelton
• 888.CAMPOUT
• parks.wa.govparks

Union

In 1889 logging pioneer John McReavy platted Union City along Hood Canal's steep southern shore. From 1924 until it burned in 1952 Union was home to the state's first artist colony, Olympus Manor, which drew painters, musicians, writers, sculptors and dancers to the area. Today there's a marina - and spectacular views of the Olympics.

McReavy House

The house isn't much to see (yet); it's being refurbished to exhibit artifacts from pioneer families, the Skokomish Tribe, and Olympus Manor. Website has local arts and culture events.
• 10 E 2nd St.
• mcreavyhouse.org

Union Paddle and Row

Human powered watercraft for all ages: stand up paddle boards, kayaks, water bikes, and a variety of rowboats including wherrys. Local kayak tours by request.
• 5130 E State Route 106
• 360.359.3308
• unionpaddleandrow.com

Pier Peer: Evening Explorations of Sea Life on Hood Canal

People for Puget Sound offers a family-friendly night exploration of Hood Canal with marine naturalists talking about the animals attracted to underwater lights. Some are weird. Dates vary. • 5101 E State Route 106 • 360.754.9177
• pugetsound.org/events

Pebble Beach Place

Two bedroom, one bath vacation bungalow among cedar trees with view of the Canal. Enjoy private beach, hot tub, and nearby wooded trails. • 10230 E State Route 106
• 206.550.5962
• pebblebeachplace.com

Hunter Gardens

Family owned and operated farm since 1880's. Includes a general store, plant nursery,pumpkin patch and pre-cut and u-cut Christmas trees. Limited hours in winter.
• 1921 E State Route 106
• 360.898.2222
• hunter-farms.com

Twanoh State Park

Park buildings constructed by Civilian Conservation Corps in 1930's are tucked into woods along the beach. Chum salmon in Twanoh Creek; loggers' springboard notches in cedars along the 2.5-mile trail. Year-round camping, shellfish harvesting, boat ramp, and moorage. Day-use Discover Pass required. • 12190 E State Route 106
• moorage: 360.902.8844
• parks.wa.gov/parks

Alderbrook Resort & Spa

Simple, elegant rooms and guesthouses on Hood Canal surrounded by large grassy areas to lounge or play. Enclosed pool, outdoor fire pit and fine dining all with water and Olympics views. Moorage available.
• 7101 E State Route 106
• alderbrookresort.com

Alderbrook Golf Club

Open year round, the course offers rolling fairways bordered by massive evergreen and fir trees. Clubhouse includes restaurant and bar.
• 3330 Country Club Dr. E
• 360.898.2560
• alderbrookgolf.com

Historic Water Tour of Lower Hood Canal

The *Lady Alderbrook* cruises Hood Canal with an historian as guide. Summer schedules vary. • 7101 E State Route 106 • 360.898.2200
• alderbrookresort.com

Robinhood Restaurant and Pub

Built in 1934. Offers Northwest cuisine, vegetarian and vegan options, and "farm-to-plate" offerings from local High Water Farm. Live music.
• 6790 E State Route 106
• 360.898.4400
• therobinhood.com

Hood Canal Adventures

Guided kayaking, fishing, crabbing, geocaching, and hiking tours available. Kayak, paddle board, paddle boat, motor boat and party barge rentals. Open daily in summer. Reservations required.
• Alderbrook Resort Dock • 7101 E State Route 106 • 360.898.2628
• hoodcanaladventures.com

Harmony Hill Retreat Center

Nonprofit retreat facility is focused on healthy living and offers retreats for individuals, couples, and families; health and wellness events. Calendar lists programs and yoga classes. • 7362 E State Route 106
• 360.898.2363
• harmonyhill.org

Shelton

The county seat and most populous town, Shelton is home to a wide range of services. Several spots are attractive to visitors.

Sage Books

Focused on fiction, children's lit and Northwest-icana; coffee bar and a nice little cafe. This is a warm, hang-out kind of place, with helpful staff. • 116 W Railroad Ave.
• 360.426.6011
• sagebookstore.com

Xinh's Clam and Oyster House

Named for the chef/owner, a former Vietnam mess cook, West Coast champion oyster shucker and creator of some lovely seafood stew. Little beef but it's easy to eat vegetarian here. • 221 W Railroad Ave. • 360.427.8709
• xinhsrestaurant.com

Octopus Garden

I'd like to be...a small jewelry and gift shop. Run by the Timmermans, goldsmiths and designers, the Garden also shows pieces by area artists.
• 123 W Railroad Ave.
• 360.426.1280
• octopusgardenjewelry.com

Olympic Bakery and Deli

Serves fresh breads, cookies and desserts, plus soups, sandwiches, Olympic Mountain ice cream. Carries an impressive collection of wine and cheese.
• 591 E Pickering Rd. • 360.426.4566
• olympicbakery.com

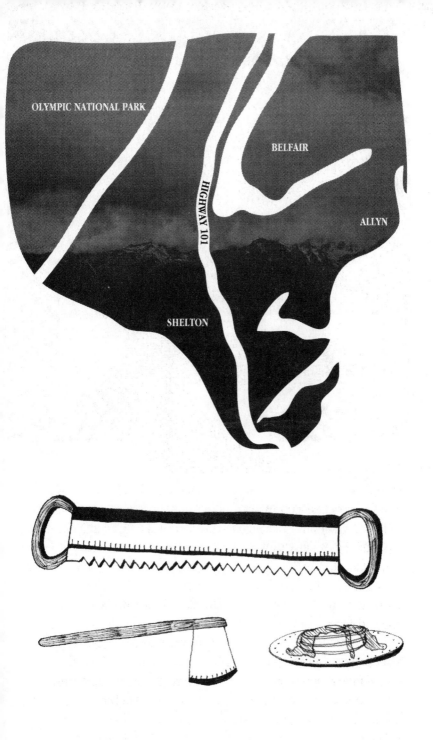

Afterword

In 1792 George Vancouver sailed his ten-gun survey ship into Commencement Bay. The British expedition marked the first time South Puget Sound was explored by Europeans. Vancouver named the inlet Puget's Sound, for his lieutenant, Peter Puget.

So what? Vancouver didn't discover the damn place. By the time his crew dropped anchor, the Suquamish, Duwamish, Nisqually, Snoqualmie, and Muckleshoot had been here some 12,000 years, if you believe the Bering Strait land-bridge theorists. Or maybe, as Salish legend tells us, the first people were dropped here at the end of Myth Time, by a supernatural being called Snoqualm, the Changer. One version is only incrementally stranger than the other.

The Europeans who ended up here are the same ones who didn't click with the Old World, so they came through Ellis Island to New York. Then they realized they didn't fit in with the East Coast crowd, so they headed west until they reached our shores. Our founders were the fringe of the fringe, but they felt at home among the Doug firs and mountain peaks. Those trees and mountains became their skyscrapers— grander than anything the East Coast or Europe had to offer.

Some of them specifically chose the South Sound. They cleared stumps and built cities. Boomtowns that evolved into something different than the rest of the Northwest. We're still different. This isn't Seattle. We have fewer global brands, less media attention, and we're not so slick.

I had lunch with a Seattle friend the other day. He's a self-described restaurateur—which is a Seattle way of saying he owns a bar and a couple of overpriced pizza joints. With a backhanded compliment, he said, "Oh, I love Tacoma. I'd live there, except it doesn't have a scene." "Funny," I said, "that's precisely why I *do* live there."

When people talk about the South Sound, they like to throw around the word authenticity. Let's take it a step further. We're not only comfortable with who we are; we have undeniable attitude about it. We have locally-grown, handcrafted chips on our shoulders. True South Sounders can't help but say, "Hell yes, I'm from Tacoma—or Lakewood, or Oly—you have a problem with that?"

But South Sounders have more than just attitude. We've got pristine waterfront, towering woods and ancient mountains. We live in historic homes, work in high-tech offices, and fish from glacier-fed rivers. Our beaches are still full of life and our heads are even fuller with ideas. South Sound chefs, writers, artists, teachers, and business leaders can not only stand toe-to-toe with any talents in the world, but can also kick a little ass when they need to. We run the range from rabid conservatives to kooky liberals, but we'll still gather around a bonfire at the beach and sing songs together. We're not even afraid to argue about religion. Maybe that's because we're more aware of our souls than other folks.

Or maybe that's because this is a soul place. From where I sit right now, I can look out a single window and see the connected waters of the Puget Sound and the misty top of Mount Rainier. That kind of perspective humbles us. But not too much. We still know we're something special.

Tom Llewllyn

Tom Llewellyn *is author of "The Tilting House" and commits guerilla art as part of Beautiful Angle.*

181

Contributors

Ron Swarner is the publisher of the *Weekly Volcano*. He's been adrift since the breakup of Wham.

Tom Llewellyn writes words in books and on posters and gets very little sleep. Tomllewellyn.blogspot.com

Laura Anderson is the Guide's public relations manager. A recent graduate of Santa Clara University, she's versed in the worlds of public relations and bartending (which are not as different as they may first appear). Laura also has unconditional love for yoga, stuffed animals and the musical talents of John Mayer.

Chris Sharp created the broad shape of the Guide. He paints on canvas and on signs, and won the Greater Tacoma Community Foundation's inaugural "Foundations of Art" award.

Meri Arnett-Kremian is a life artistry coach, a family law attorney who believes in the collaborative process and a writer. She's published legal analysis and poetry, and blogs regularly. Her work is anthologized in Invoking the Scribes of Ancient Egypt and in upcoming work by graduates of the UW's memoir certificate program. Contact: finallyme.com

C. Rosalind Bell writes, cooks and farms in her yard. Contact: rosalindbell.blogspot.com

Barb Bourscheidt specializes in writing about her food, gardening and travel adventures. Ms Bourscheidt maintains a regular blog, busybarbsblog. blogspot.com, and can be reached at barbbourscheidt@yahoo.com

Carolyn Burt, M.Ed.: writer, artist; owner, Proctor Art Gallery LLC; educator; born and raised in Tacoma; B.A. and M.Ed. in administration from University of Puget Sound. Contact: carolynburtstudio.com

Courtenay Chamberlin: communications consultant, runner, reader, gardener, mother, bit of a beer and coffee snob. Contact: cwc@harbornet.com

Alec Clayton writes for the *Weekly Volcano* and other area publications. Contact info: alec@alecclayton.com

Erica Lynn Coe lives in McKinley Hill and enjoys dining and shopping at neighborhood businesses. Erica_coe@hotmail.com

J. Shawn Cole is a freelance contributor with a passion for dance, volunteering and being a mom. Contact: imjsc@harbornet.com

Jackie Fender is a mother of three and a Tacoma creative culture enthusiast. Always with pen or camera in hand. Contact: jacksfender@yahoo.com.

Molly Gilmore is a writer, editor and teacher of Soul Motion™. contact:inthedance@gmail.com

John Hines teaches history, loves Tacoma and writes to share his passion for both. Contact: jhhines57@gmail.com

John Idstrom blogs about food and life from his perch on the lip of Puget Gulch. Read his posts at www.meezenplace.com or contact him directly at johnidstrom@gmail.com.

L. Lisa Lawrence is an award-winning writer and photographer; her work appears in every issue of *South Sound Magazine*. contact: wildcelti-crose.net

Tara Mattina is communications director for the Port of Tacoma.

Jesse Michener is a hometown Tacoman, photographer and videographer, writer, mother of a small tribe of girls. Contact: jessemichener.com

Dawn Quinn has resided in the Hilltop neighborhood of Tacoma since 2007, has been vegan for seven years and started writing at six. She's a freelance writer and runs the vegan food blog VeganMoxie.com, where she can be contacted.

Carmen Sterba: a Washingtonian who taught in Japan and writes non-fiction and haiku. Contact: Carmen.sterba@cptc.edu

Sharon Styer: writer, photographer, explorer and lover of projects both large and small. Contact: Sharon@sharonstyer.com

Kim Thompson: visit Kim (a.k.a. Gritty City Woman) at grittycitywoman.com, on Facebook, twitter and Pinterest.

Kate Albert Ward regularly shows her hometown-love by writing and editing for the Tacoma-centric www.PostDefiance.com. Contact: kate.albert.ward@postdefiance.com

Rebecca Young is a long-time journalist who has lived in Tacoma since 1992. Contact: rebeccayoungbooks.com

Brutus Beafcoque is a hiker and naturalist from Tacoma, Washington.

Ken Miller was born in Brooklyn, grew up in California and has lived in Tacoma for 40 years. He's worked in corporate and small business, community organizing and nonprofits. Ken writes, consults and teaches on topics related to strategy and organization alignment. His novel about Somali pirates is in development as a feature film.

Sean Alexander is one of Tacoma's wily creatives. His past projects have included The Helm Gallery and The Squeak and Squawk Music Festival. His drawing work has been exhibited around the country and appeared in a variety of periodicals. His goal is to always write, draw, perform, and organize with a sense of purpose. He is absolutely dialed-in and hopelessly clumsy.

Acknowledgments

First we want to acknowledge a big debt: Richard Saul Wurman's break-through in information design, the Access guides. The Access series orga-nizes information geographically and uses maps, icons, drawings and text to deliver information. Our Guide wouldn't exist without Mr. Wurman's insights.

The Guide began as a Kickstarter project, which made it possible for people all over the world to be involved. Not only is Kickstarter a great site; the Brooklyn team was quite helpful, answering even dumb questions quickly and clearly.

But we didn't have to go global for partners. Lots of South Sounders stepped up, spreading the word, offering suggestions, introducing us to new resources.

Regardless of their coordinates, all these people and organizations helped make the Guide possible. And this means we met an important goal: to weave new threads through our sense of community.

THANK YOU!!!

Brian Forth and SiteCrafting Inc.
Greater Tacoma Community Foundation
Port of Tacoma
Jeffrey Helsdon
Broadway Center for the Performing Arts
Dale and Joanna Chesnut
Angela and Jack Connelly
City of Lakewood
Exit 133
Metro Parks Tacoma
Museum of Glass
Office of Tacoma Mayor Marilyn Strickland
John Stumpf
Janet Thiessen
Derek Young
Jocko Burks
Bill and Ann Evans
Ed Grogan
Jennifer Irwin
Mark Lewington
Amy McBride
Willmar Moe
Greg and Lynne Roberts
Stanley Schmidtke
Ron Swarner
Kate Albert Ward
Jamie and Sally Will
Martha Wilson

R.J. Adler
Jessica Alexander
Don Anderson
Dave and Linda Anderson
Benjamin Anderstone
E. Archambeault
Laurie Arnold
John k. Atwill
Darren Baker
Steve and Mary Barger
The Beams
Brady Bekker
Andrew Belcher
Sharon Benson
Hannah Bergland
Mike Betz
Benji Bittle
Linda Blair
Arianna Bodaghi
Mary Boone
Mary Brace
RebeccaBuchert
Janice Brevik
Frances Buckmaster
Valerie Burns
Carolyn Burt
Mariesa Bus
Justin Camarata
Candis Carbone
Courtenay Chamberlin
Laurie Cinotto
Constance Claussen
Halley Clugbucket Griffin
Isaiah Coberly
Erica Coe
Rich Coker
Dick and Linda Craig
Gail Cramer
Thad Curtz
Linda Danforth
Nancy Davis
Jennifer Dawson-Miller
Dick Dorsett
Nancy Delacour
Allen Dennison
Steph Derosa
Lynn Di Nino
Sherry Douceur
Lin Eastman
Laura Edgar
Dave Edwards
Susan Eidenschink
Cathy Elford
Amber Englund
Rachel Ervin
Gregg Peter Farah
Timothy Farrell
Jackie Fender
Ben Ferguson
HeideFernandez-Llamazares
Kathleen Figetakis
Dennis Flannigan

Jen Flood
Lynda Foster
Bengt Freepons
Becky Frehse
Andrew Fry
Laura Gardner
Marcia Garrett
Michael Garrity
Jessica Gavre
Wayne Gilham
Amy and Calvin Goings
Melissa Goldman
Casandra Gorell
Jon Graef
Mary Grant
Brenda Groboski
Jake Guadnola
Erin Guinup
Cynthia Hammer
Jamie Hammon
Diane Knuckey Hansen
Dan Hansen
Scott Haydon
Susan Hayes
Peggy Heim
Corrinne Henderson
Randy Herbon
Becky Hester
Kelly Hill
Galen Hon
Mark and Eileen Hudak
Dan Hulse
Denny Hunthausen
Linda Hutcheson
Andrew Hyde
John K. Idstrom
Terese Jackson
Laurie Jinkins
Taylor Jones
Sarah Jones
Deborah Jordan
Nadya Kadrevis
Amy Kamp
Dmitri and Lisa Keating
Ruth Keller
Brian Kerr
Eugene Kester
Roy Kimbel
Marilyn Kimmerling
Chris King
Steve King
Michelle Kinney
Tim Knudson
Heather Koch
Kathy Koch
Dan Koch Construction
Diane Koch
Marcy Kulland and TerryVirgona
Nathe and Alicia Lawver
Deb Layton
Emily Lenzi
Monique Letourneau

Dorothy Lewis
Carolyn Linden
Bonnie Lindstrom
Julie Lingenfelter Kiessel
Kathleen Lio
Tom Llewellyn
Karin Losk
Courtney N. Love
Matt Lynn
Kevin Manley
Victoria Martinez
James Matteucci
Tara Mattina
Andrew McCaffrey
J.J. McCament
Resa McCane
John K. McCluskey
Helen McGovern
Margy McGroarty
Kacie McKinney
Maija McKnight
Timothy McNeely
Jessica Meier
Ryan Mello
Patricia Menzies
Marisa Mezs
Jeremy Monin
Mark Monlux
Barb Montro
Janet Muelhans
Kerry Muise
Noel Murphy
Julie Myers
Jodi Nelson
Darren Nerland
Scott Neste
Susan Newsom
Judith Nilan
Gregg Peter Nordlund
Matt Oberfield
Michael Ogura
Ronald Oldham
Chandler O'Leary
Nancy Pare
Mary Pascoe
Jamie Paulson
Mallory Pernaa
Clare Petrich
Sandi Phillips
George Pilant
Alisa Pisciotta
Dawn Quinn
Carol Lee Ragus
Scott Ramsey
Lane Rasberry
Jordan Rash
Christy Reedy
Karl Reinsch
Mark Reutlinger
Jim Roberts
Carol Robinson
Jacob Rodenbucher

Lilith Rogers
Kenny Rowe
Tad Saine
Jennifer Schaal
David Schimer
Mary Schmidtke
Megan Schrader
David Seago
Stan Selden
Peter Serko
Bruce Sharer
Charlene J. Sharp
Pat Shuman
Ana Maria Sierra
Taylor Sizemore
Clare Sleeter
RIch and Beverly Smaby
Nadine Smaby
Heather Smith
Karen Smitherman
Rebecca Solverson
Jessica Spring
Pam Sprowl
Zach Stednick
Heidi Stoermer
Heather R. Straub
Naomi Strom-Avila
Sharon Styer
Terri Swier
Mike Sylvanus
James Tallman
Sam Talluto
Carrie Tennison
Amie Thao
Alex Thomson
Susan Tompkins
Douglas Tooley
Cheryl Trooskin-Zoller
Ollie Tumelius
Keith Tyler
Heather Valtee
Jen Draper and Chris Van Vechten
Karin Van Vleck
Dan Voelpel
Lauren Walker
Ingrid Walker
Art Wang
Debra Warmington
Barry Watson
Megan Weigley
Carolyn Weisz
Ted and Janet Werner
Lani White
Rosemarie Wiegman
Karen Willard
Suzy Willhoft
David L. Wilson
James Bruce Wilson VII
LaTasha Wortham
Laura Wulf
Marguerite Yoshikawa
Leslie Young

Alexmery
Amy
Andrea
Carl
Dawn
Hannah
Jay
Jillian
Jim
Kodi
Mark
Morgan
Nathab
Patricia
Pete
Rachel
Shari
Shawllady
Tricia
Vfive

Index

The index is separated into sections that group features alphabetically-based on kind. Each feature includes a letter indicating which county it is in (P = Pierce, T = Thurston, M = Mason) and the page number.

Thanks to **Patrick Thiessen** for his indexing help. Patrick, like many of us, likes to have the last word. Here it is, Patrick: **word.**

NOTES:

NOTES:

NOTES:

NOTES:

NOTES: